Northrop Frye

Twayne's World Authors Series

Canadian Literature

Robert Lecker, Editor
McGill University

TWAS 806

Northrop Frye, *photograph courtesy Roy Nicholls*.

Northrop Frye

By Ian Balfour

York University

Twayne Publishers

A Division of G. K. Hall & Co. • *Boston*

Northrop Frye
Ian Balfour

Copyright 1988 by G. K. Hall & Co.
All rights reserved.
Published by Twayne Publishers
A Division of G. K. Hall & Co.
70 Lincoln Street
Boston, Massachusetts 02111

Copyediting supervised by Barbara Sutton
Book production by Gabrielle B. McDonald
Book design by Barbara Anderson

Typeset in 11 pt. Garamond
by Compset, Inc., Beverly, Massachusetts

Printed on permanent/durable acid-free paper
and bound in the United States of America

Library of Congress Cataloging-in-Publication Data

Balfour, Ian.
 Northrop Frye / by Ian Balfour.
   p. cm.—(Twayne's world authors series ; TWAS 806. Canadian
literature)
 Bibliography: p.
 Includes index.
 ISBN 0-8057-8235-4 (alk. paper)
 1. Frye, Northrop. I. Title. II. Series: Twayne's world authors
series ; TWAS 806. III. Series: Twayne's world authors series.
Canadian literature.
PN75.F7B27   1988
801'.95'0924—dc19   88-14680
                                                          CIP

To my mother and father

Contents

About the Author

Ian Balfour was born in Ottawa, grew up in Montreal, and received his B.A. in French and German literature from York University. He did graduate work at the University of Toronto and the Universität Tübingen, and received his Ph.D. in comparative literature from Yale University. Following his graduation from Yale, he was a postdoctoral fellow in English and a lecturer in comparative literature at Princeton University. He has published essays and reviews on Frye, romanticism, and literary theory, and is finishing a forthcoming study, *The Rhetoric of Romantic Prophecy*. Professor Balfour is a member of the English Department at York University.

Preface

Northrop Frye's inclusion in a series on "world authors" is itself a vindication of one of his critical principles. Much current thought about literature is still dominated by a romantic mythology that sharply divides the creative author from the parasitic critic; the former is thought to be original and vital, the latter derivative and deadly. But "creativity," Frye observes, "is not a property of genre." A work of fiction or poetry is not creative in any important sense simply because it is supposed to issue from the writer's imagination. Nor is literary criticism merely derivative because it presupposes a prior body of texts on which it comments. Critical or "secondary" literature loses much of its "derivative" status in relation to literature when one recognizes, with Frye, that "poems come from other poems." In some sense, everything in Western literature after Homer and the Bible is "secondary literature." In the context of the present study, both "primary" and "secondary" literature are best conceived simply as writing. The preeminence of Frye as a literary critic, though, does have something to do with qualities of his prose traditionally prized in literary aesthetics: wit and elegance of presentation, an assured sense of form and genre, to say nothing of sheer intelligence.

Northrop Frye is by common consent one of the most important literary critics and theorists of the twentieth century, and his *Anatomy of Criticism* is thought by many to be the most significant achievement of literary theory in our time. Certainly he is the foremost proponent of archetypal or myth criticism of literary texts. His work has provoked a considerable body of commentary, some of it excellent, though the present critical exposition is, to my knowledge, the first full-length study of the whole range of his works. Robert Denham's *Northrop Frye and Critical Method* focuses almost exclusively on the *Anatomy*, and its publication in 1978 predates Frye's work of the last decade. My own study devotes considerable space to *Fearful Symmetry*, which I take to be of an importance almost equal to that of the *Anatomy*, though its circumscribed topic, the poetry of William Blake, has of necessity not gained it as wide an audience. As I argue in chapter 1, Blake's work is crucial for Frye's theory of literature, not simply for the exigencies of practical criticism. Thus I dwell in that chapter as much on Blake's

poetic theory and practice, as I do on Frye's commentary. I also devote
a full chapter to Frye's writings on Canadian culture, texts that are not
well known outside of Canada, though they are of signal importance
to Frye's career. The chapters of this study are for the most part not
arranged chronologically because Frye's career does not lend itself to a
narrative of changing interests nor to a pattern of development: his
work unfolds rather than evolves.

It is not possible to deal at length with Frye's prodigious output of
more than twenty books and dozens of shorter writings. Thus even the
chapters that are organized by topic typically take a single book as the
guiding thread, though always with an eye to relevant texts from elsewhere in Frye's corpus. In attempting to do justice to the broad range
of Frye's work, I have deliberately resisted the pursuit of a single overarching thesis. I have, however, tried throughout to situate Frye's
theoretical and practical production in relation to more contemporary
criticism, especially with regard to material written after the *Anatomy*.
I believe that such a line of inquiry suggests that while the vogue of
archetypal criticism may have seen its day, the problems Frye poses are
still very much with us. Indeed Frye anticipates many of the positions
that sometimes seem to be moving "beyond" his work: his theoretical
program, in particular, continues to present a challenge for the future
of literary criticism.

                                                            Ian Balfour
York University

Acknowledgments

I am grateful to the Social Sciences and Humanities Research Council of Canada for providing indirect assistance for this project, through doctoral and postdoctoral fellowships. Jane Widdicombe was very helpful, especially with bibliographical matters, as was the excellent staff of the E. J. Pratt Library at Victoria College in Toronto. In a more general way, I am grateful to my teachers who helped put me in a position to write this book, especially Paul de Man, Cyrus Hamlin, and Northrop Frye. To Pat Parker I am indebted for the title of my third chapter, among other things. Tom Keenan read with care an earlier version of the manuscript and made many suggestions for its improvement. Deborah Esch was an exemplary in-house reader, providing critical commentary and hyperbolic encouragement when it was most needed.

Chronology

1912	H. Northrop Frye born in Sherbrooke, Quebec, 14 July.
1929	Enrolled at Victoria College, University of Toronto.
1933	Graduates first in the Honours Course in Philosophy and English. Later enrolls at Emmanuel College, University of Toronto, to study theology.
1936	Ordained as minister of the United Church of Canada. Studies for B.A. in English literature at Merton College, Oxford.
1937	Marries Helen Kemp.
1938	Lecturer in English at Victoria College, University of Toronto.
1947	*Fearful Symmetry.* Becomes professor of English, Victoria College.
1948–1952	Editor of *Canadian Forum.*
1957	*Anatomy of Criticism.*
1959–1966	Principal of Victoria College.
1963	*The Well-Tempered Critic, The Educated Imagination. T. S. Eliot,* and *Fables of Identity.*
1965	*A Natural Perspective: Essays on the Development of Shakespearean Comedy and Romance* and *The Return of Eden: Five Essays on Milton's Epics.*
1967	*Fools of Time: Studies in Shakespearean Tragedy* and *The Modern Century.* Appointed the first University Professor at the University of Toronto.
1968–1977	*A Study of English Romanticism.* Member of the Canadian Radio-Television and Telecommunications Commission.
1970	*The Stubborn Structure: Essays on Criticism and Society.*
1971	*The Bush Garden: Essays on the Canadian Imagination* and *The Critical Path: An Essay on the Social Context of Literary Criticism.*

1975   Charles Eliot Norton Professor of Poetry, Harvard University.

1976   *The Secular Scripture: A Study of the Structure of Romance* and *Spiritus Mundi: Essays on Literature, Myth, and Society.* President of the Modern Language Association.

1978   *Northrop Frye on Culture and Literature: A Collection of Review Essays.* Appointed Chancellor of Victoria University.

1980   *Creation and Recreation.*

1982   *The Great Code: The Bible and Literature* and *Divisions on a Ground: Essays on Canadian Culture.*

1983   *The Myth of Deliverance: Reflections on Shakespeare's Problem Comedies.*

1986   *Northrop Frye on Shakespeare.* Death of Helen Kemp Frye.

Chapter One
The Myths of Poetry: Beginnings and Blake

Rarely has a young critic made as impressive an entrance onto the literary scene as Northrop Frye did in 1947 with the publication of *Fearful Symmetry*, his path-breaking study of the poetry and thought of William Blake. Until then the great critical intelligence of Northrop Frye had been something of a Canadian secret. Most of his writings had been published in the *Canadian Forum*, a journal of high quality but one lacking a broad international readership. *Fearful Symmetry* was not only to change the shape of Blake studies for generations, it would also become the inaugural example of what was soon to be codified as "archetypal" or "myth" criticism. Frye's first major work heralded a change in the course of literary criticism and theory, not unlike the poetic revolution effected by his subject, William Blake.

Northrop Frye was born on 14 July 1912 in Sherbrooke, Quebec. His early education, strongly encouraged by his family, was liberal and catholic. By the time he arrived as a freshman at Victoria College in the University of Toronto, he was already well-versed in several literatures and languages. Anecdotes still circulate about fellow students so intimidated by the extraordinary scope of his learning that some even dropped out of college in despair. Frye placed first in his class every year during his university career, earning in 1933 a B.A. in the Honours Program in Philosophy and English Literature. He then entered Emmanuel College at Victoria, where he was trained in the ministry of the United Church, after which he was duly ordained in 1936. His first position included riding on horseback through the wilds of Saskatchewan to attend to his charges. It was not long, however, before Frye realized he was better suited for the podium than the pulpit, and he subsequently went to Merton College, Oxford to pursue a bachelor's degree in English literature. His studies at Oxford were interrupted briefly by a year's teaching at Victoria College. Upon finishing his Oxford B.A. after a further year of study in 1938–39, Frye returned

to Toronto and Victoria College to take up a position as assistant professor of English at his alma mater, where he has remained on the
faculty ever since. Though Frye has on occasion taught as a visiting
professor at Princeton, Harvard, and elsewhere, Toronto has been for
him a still point in the turning academic world. While teaching full
time, Frye has been active in several other capacities: among them
editor of the *Canadian Forum* from 1948 to 1952, principal of Victoria
College from 1959 to 1966, member of the Canadian Radio-Television
and Communications Commission from 1968 to 1977, and president
of the Modern Language Association in 1976. Frye went well beyond
the call of duty for a literary critic and in doing so contributed much
to cultural and intellectual life inside and outside of Canada.

The simple facts of Frye's life, then, are hardly the stuff of which
great biographies are made. Indeed, Frye has sometimes remarked that
his life was deliberately organized so that no one could possibly write
a biography of it. As a critic, he almost religiously avoided biographical inquiry as an approach to the understanding of texts; this is precisely the appropriate strategy for an analysis of his own work. The
present study will concentrate on an exposition and critical assessment
of his writings, the real foundation of his significance and enduring
interest.

Frye's first book, *Fearful Symmetry,* is a rarity among the initial pub-
lications of academic critics, since it never went through a phase as a
doctoral dissertation. Such projects usually bear the marks of a specialized scholarship considered appropriate for an apprentice of the
trade. But *Fearful Symmetry* is a vast, sprawling work that is little concerned with "scholarship," narrowly conceived. Frye seeks through this
work not so much to make a contribution to Blake studies as to revo-
lutionize our understanding of poetry as such, with Blake singled out
as the exemplary poet.

Fearful Symmetry divides into three parts, "The Argument," "The
Development of the Symbolism," and "The Final Synthesis," though
it might well have been divided in two: the first part sketches the
theoretical foundations of different aspects of Blake's poetry and
thought with texts culled from the entire corpus, whereas the second
and third parts offer extended commentaries, in roughly chronological
order, on all of Blake's major works and many of his minor ones.[1] What
is striking about the texture of Frye's commentary is the relative absence of close readings of specific passages, of the kind familiar to students trained in the tradition of New Criticism. One of New

Criticism's foremost practitioners has written of the "heresy of paraphrase," and paraphrase emerges as one of the dominant modes of Frye's commentary, almost as if *Fearful Symmetry* were an immense translation of Blake's works.[2] "Paraphrase," writes Paul de Man

is, of course, the mainstay of all critical writing. It is generally, though not necessarily, shorter than the text it claims to elucidate, but what is certain is that it can never be the same. It is always a transposition, a translation. . . . It proceeds by a complex and, in the case of a skillful reader, subtle strategy of expansion and elision, the most important being not so much what one develops, makes explicit and repeats, but what one omits. The principle of omission is usually quite simple: one omits what one does not understand.[3]

But Frye is rarely guilty, in his expansive work on Blake, of sins of omission. Occasionally, in his desire to formulate a consistent mythology appropriate for the entire Blake canon, Frye will opt for one of several interpretive possibilities and cover with his tracks the paths not taken. On the whole, however, Frye's paraphrasing commentary is remarkably comprehensive, and only rarely displays the character of compromise: he explains rather than explains away the manifest difficulties of Blake's texts. But Frye's prose, in its turn, presents difficulties of its own. His penchant for paradox often results in the restatement of a complexity in Blake's work rather than a domestication of it. At times the line between Frye's own thought and his exposition of Blake's is so fine as to be indistinguishable, much to the consternation of some of his critics.[4] It is almost as if Frye, rather like Blake in his epic *Milton,* merges with the subject of his writing and speaks in that double persona. Often statements made by Frye in explicating Blake are read as if they were Frye's own credo, which is by no means always the case, despite his great sympathy for Blake's poetic project. This "confusion," however, is a problem primarily for those who read with the design of discerning in the text the embodiment of a single authorial intention, a practice that Frye himself will rightly call into question.

Prior to the appearance of *Fearful Symmetry,* it was not uncommon to think of William Blake as either a madman or a mystic: an inspired poet, perhaps, but not an author with the stature of Wordsworth, Shelley, or the other major romantics with whom he is sometimes grouped.[5] Several important figures of the late nineteenth century were enthusiastic about Blake's achievement: Swinburne, for example, authored a book-length essay on Blake, and Yeats coedited a three-volume edition of his works in 1893. Yeats's opinion could command considerable respect, but the judgment of so distinguished a poet (who, after all, claimed to converse with fairies) remained somewhat eccentric. Blake's dubious position in the canon of English literature persisted well into the twentieth century, with the question of the coherence of his poetry very much an open one.

It was against the chaotic composite drawing painted by Blake's critics that Frye set out to show the extraordinarily systematic character of the poet's work: its fearful symmetry. In Frye's view Blake was, more than most poets, a "victim of anthologies." He had been read primarily for the brief, deceptively simple lyrics from the *Songs of Innocence and of Experience,* to the neglect of his longer, gnomic works known as the "Prophetic Books," texts that constitute by far the greater part of his poetic production. The working hypothesis of *Fearful Symmetry* is that Blake's poems form a unified corpus, a single immense "body" of work, to take up the Blakean metaphor wholeheartedly adopted by Frye.

Where does one turn to begin to understand Blake's monumental corpus? In a sense, one does not "turn" at all, for, as Frye asserts: "Blake's poems are poems, and must be studied as such" (*FS,* 6). He insists that "any attempt to explain them in terms of something that is not poetry is bound to fail" (*FS,* 6). It would seem hard to imagine any disagreement with the tautological statement that "poems are poems," based as it is on the identity principle of logic as well as common sense. Yet Frye's claim has something polemical and even scandalous about it. Blake's poems are not to be considered literary versions of any extralinguistic referent: a poem does not illustrate anything that is not already itself poetic. This does not imply that a poem should be read in utter isolation, in a "vacuum," as it is sometimes phrased. Frye, like nature, abhors a vacuum: a poem's real context is its literary one, and thus poems themselves must be the framework of any poetic analysis. Knowledge derived from disciplines such as psychology, history, anthropology, or sociology is, at best, of indirect help in the study of literature.

From the opening pages of *Fearful Symmetry,* it is apparent that the reader is not simply engaging one more book to take its place among others in the circumscribed field of Blake studies. *Fearful Symmetry* is at once a major work of practical and theoretical criticism; practical insofar as it offers detailed interpretations of specific poems, theoretical insofar as it examines Blake's work as "an illustration of the poetic process" (*FS,* Preface). This entails nothing less than a general theory of poetry, with Blake's poems regarded as the exemplary instances. Much is at stake for the course of Frye's criticism in adopting such a strategy, as the transitions from particular to general, and individual to universal, are not always self-evident or unproblematic. Readers may well wonder whether there is such a thing as "the poetic process," a universal grammar, rhetoric, and logic common to all poets at all times. Equally questionable may be the status of Blake as the exemplary poet, for he is often considered to have written in a veritable "private language." Though the notion of a private language or symbolism is itself ultimately a contradiction in terms—and Frye will demonstrate its inappropriateness in Blake's case—the suspicion may still linger that Blake is too eccentric a writer, too far removed from the beaten path to stand as an exemplar of poetry itself.

Such questions cannot be answered without examining what Blake calls "minute particulars," which in *Fearful Symmetry* is the substance of Frye's commentary and criticism, even if those particulars are themselves often of a general nature. Two kinds of general principles can be distinguished: those pertaining to literature and those pertaining to criticism. The latter are more pervasive and less problematic since, in some ways, it is relatively easy to formulate certain general guidelines applicable to the understanding of any poem whatsoever. However, to generalize about the poetic process based on the work of a single poet is a much more demanding task, perhaps all the more so in Blake's case, since it is attended by the irony of the poet's own warning that: "To Generalize is to be an idiot."[6]

No author, of course, is necessarily the ablest critic of his or her own work. As Frye would later write: "Wordsworth's Preface to the *Lyrical Ballads* is a remarkable document, but as a piece of Wordsworthian criticism, nobody would give it more than about a B plus."[7] Blake, on the other hand, is "a poet whose poems were quite consistent with a theory of poetry" (*FS*, 147). More specifically with respect to Blake's symbolism, Frye accepts the poet's formulation of the nature of sublime poetry as appropriate for his own work: "Allegory addressed to Intellectual Powers while it is altogether hidden from the Corporeal Understanding, is my Definition of the Most Sublime Poetry; it is also somewhat in the same manner defined by Plato."[8] The greatest poetry may well be allegorical, but what then is allegory? The word itself derives from the Greek *allos,* meaning other, and *agourein,* meaning to speak, especially in the "agora" or marketplace, that is to say, in public. (The term allegory replaced an older Greek work, *hyponoia,* used

to denote hidden meaning or thought.)⁹ Allegory, in short, means
something other than what it says. Hence the necessity of criticism to
paraphrase or translate from the allegorical surface of the text to what
is supposed to be its meaning. Blake's valorization of allegory is a minority opinion among English romantics as well as among many twentieth-century critics steeped in romantic doctrine. The most influential
statement of the dominant view is Coleridge's, who claims that
allegory

is but a Translation of abstract notions into a picture-language which is itself
nothing but an abstraction from the objects of the senses; the principal being
more worthless even than its phantom proxy, both alike unsubstantial, and
the former shapeless to boot. On the other hand a Symbol (*ho estin aei taute-
gorikon*) is characterized by a translucence of the Special in the Individual or
of the General in the Especial. Above all by the Translucence of the Eternal
in and through the Temporal. It always partakes of the Reality which it renders intelligible; and while it enunciates the whole, abides itself as a living
part in that Unity, of which it is the representative.¹⁰

It would seem difficult to choose allegory over symbol in Coleridge's
stark dichotomy, for who would not prefer substance over shadow,
plenitude over emptiness, light over darkness, indeed life over death?
Yet Coleridge's theory cannot be accepted uncritically as a viable theory
of representation. In what sense, for example, does a word *partake* of
the reality it renders intelligible, with the possible exception of the
word for "word"?¹¹ Whatever the conceptual difficulties, Coleridge
does voice a disdain of allegory shared by many of his contemporaries.
Blake himself occasionally uses the term in a sense close to Coleridge's,
as when he refers disparagingly to allegory as inferior to "vision."¹²
When Frye speaks of Blake's poetry as allegory, he uses the term in its
positive Blakean sense, as sublime poetry addressed to the intellectual
powers. Apparently when Blake reevaluated allegory in this passage
from *A Vision of the Last Judgement*, he was writing "in fetters," as Blake
says of Milton when the latter wrote of angels and of God.

    The positive character of allegory need not be overemphasized since
"allegory" for Frye is more a descriptive than an evaluative term.¹³
Allegory "is a literary language with its own idioms and its own syn-
tactical arrangement of ideas" (*FS*, 10). To characterize Blake's poetry
as allegory nonetheless poses some new problems even as it resolves
earlier ones. Frye's sympathies are clear when he writes, for example

that "Blake's tiger is allegory; the British lion is an allegory of something" (*FS,* 383). Blake's tiger is to the British lion what metaphor is to simile, an identification rather than the notation of a resemblance. But what is an allegory that cannot be "translated"; in other words, what has happened to the "other" (*allos*) of allegory? Allegory, insofar as it is a language of its own, requires translation, and presumably loses something in that translation, the transposition into meaning that is not itself allegorical. It seems then that allegorical poetry both demands and resists its own translation.

Frye regrets that "ignorance of the methods and techniques of allegorical writing is still almost universal," and suggests that if Blake were read in terms of his own theory of poetry, it would mean "the beginning of a complete revolution in one's reading of all poetry" (*FS,* 11). He is faithful, moreover, to Blake's stress on the intellectual character of allegory. The response to allegorical poetry (and that is now to say, all poetry) has little to do with impressions and feelings vaguely evoked by poems, as celebrated in certain versions of a romantic or symbolist aesthetic. Allegory is addressed to the intellectual powers and demands an appropriate response. Clearly, much is at stake for the future of poetic theory and the practice of criticism when Frye transforms Blake's judgment about the most sublime poetry into a general theory of all poetry as allegory.

In his literary commentaries, Frye rarely feels bound to respect chronology, the category that organizes so much unimaginative work in literary criticism. But two of Blake's earliest published works do constitute a brief compendium of issues that will occupy him throughout his creative life and serve Frye as a convenient introduction to the poet's thought. These series of aphorisms, entitled *There Are No Natural Religions* and *All Religions Are One,* are concerned largely with Blake's epistemology, or theory of knowledge. Frye's first chapter, "The Case Against Locke," indicates to what extent the crucial object of Blake's early polemics, both explicit and implicit, was John Locke, the seventeenth-century philosopher of empiricism, whose *Essay Concerning Human Understanding* gave an eloquent philosophical foundation to what had and has for centuries passed as common sense. For Locke, the human mind is like a blank piece of paper on which sense impressions are inscribed or, alternatively, like a "cabinet" or room that is furnished with ideas received from the senses. Sensory data in turn provide material for the other great "fountain" of knowledge, namely reflection. Locke is also a thinker who advocates reason over faith, is suspicious of "enthusiasm," or what Blake would call inspiration, and who regards metaphors and figurative language generally—the very idiom of poetic discourse—as vehicles of deception. None of these are views that would find any favor with Blake, for reasons that will become apparent.

Much closer to Blake among British philosophers is the more eccentric and idealistic George Berkeley, whose work was both a continuation and a critique of the Lockian legacy. Blake's only direct commentary on Berkeley survives in his annotations to the latter's *Siris,* a treatise on the nature of human perception and the virtues of tarwater. For Blake, Berkeley's text is primarily a point of departure for a celebration of the imagination as the "Divine Body" of Man. Frye finds elsewhere in Berkeley a doctrine that he takes as a key to unlock Blake's idea of knowledge: the doctrine expressed in the formula *esse est percipi:* "to be is to be perceived." This dictum suggests that the world is not simply a collection of distinct objects of indubitable existence independent of our perception of them: "Mental Things are alone Real," Blake claims.[14] Berkeley's formulation, *esse est percipi,* implies the perceptual and conceptual unity of subject and object. The unit of existence, for Blake, is what he alternately calls "form" or "image," and the fact that the two are interchangeable is, in Frye's view, crucial for the understanding of Blake's work, both practical and theoretical.

The dictum *esse est percipi,* taken by itself, is illuminating for a reading of Blake, but it is hardly sufficient to stand as the single motto for his epistemology. Its passive form leaves little, so to speak, to the imagination. For Blake, the imagination is the most exalted of human faculties, that which marks the human as divine. Indeed, the imagination can barely retain the name of "faculty," a category left over from so many eighteenth-century morticians of the mind. The Blakean view of the imagination as the locus of all creative activity requires that Berkeley's phrase be reformulated as *esse est percipere,* "To be is to perceive." Such phrasing goes beyond a simple identification of subject and object to identify being itself as an activity of perception. If imagination is an intensified form of perception, then the latter must stand as a lofty mode of being in the Blakean hierarchy. The quality of perception is for Blake in direct proportion to the activity of the imagination. Whereas the Lockian mind of passive perception settles for similes, the Blakean imagination demands metaphors: "What it will be Questiond When the Sun rises do you not see a round disk of fire somewhat like a Guinea O no no no I see an Innumerable company of the Heavenly host crying Holy, Holy, Holy is the Lord God Almighty. . . ."[15] More than a metaphor, Blake's figure is a personification or prosopopoeia, the rhetorical figure that comes closest to performing creation ex nihilo. Such a vision, in Blake's view as in Frye's, is imaginative rather than imaginary, an embodiment of the creative principle without which there would be neither art nor civilization. Thus the passage on the perception of the sun just quoted implies rather more than the dictum "beauty is in the eye of the beholder." It soon becomes clear how the epistemological task of overcoming the Lockian division of subject and object can be achieved in the concrete practice of art. "The work of art," as Frye writes in the spirit of Blake,

is produced by the entire imagination. The dull mind is always thinking in terms of general antitheses, and it is instructive to see how foolish these antitheses look when they are applied to art. We cannot say that painting a picture is either an intellectual or emotional act: it is obviously both at once. We cannot say that it is either a reflective or an active process: it is obviously both at once. We cannot say that it is "mental" or "bodily": no distinction between brainwork and handiwork is relevant to it. We cannot say that the picture is a product of internal choice or external compulsion, for what the painter wants to do is what he has to do. Art is based on sense experience, yet it is an imaginative ordering of sense experience: it therefore belongs neither to the "inside" or to the "outside" of the Lockian universe, but to both at once. (*FS*, 24)

It is a commonplace of romantic aesthetics, both English and continental, that the imagination mediates between the classic polarities of Western thought such as the sensible and the intellectual: Blake is distinctive chiefly for the extraordinary energy of his defense of the imagination.[16] It is no wonder then that art and the imagination, through their supposed capacity to resolve the false dichotomies of ordinary experience and our perception of it, come to occupy the central place in the architectonic, or overarching structure, of Blake's poetic thought.

Having established a preliminary framework for the understanding of Blakean theory and terminology, Frye proceeds in his second chapter, "The Rising God," to outline the narrative or mythic structure of Blake's allegorical vision. Frye's later work will go on to explore various senses of the word *myth* for literary criticism and cultural studies, but its most basic meaning for Frye, as for Aristotle, is story of plot; he rarely uses the word *myth* to denote something that is not true by virtue of its lack of correspondence to a given external referent. Even a cursory study of Blake's poetic canon shows how thoroughly pervaded it is by the myths of the Judaeo-Christian Bible: the poems are scarcely intelligible without some knowledge of their foundational text. It will be equally evident, however, that Blake adapts as much as he adopts from the biblical myths, at least insofar as they are commonly understood.

The story of the Fall offers the most striking example of Blake's imaginative rereading of the Bible. The biblical account, in its most common interpretation, narrates the seduction of Eve by Satan, the subsequent seduction of Adam by Eve, and the consequent expulsion from Eden, a paradise where the parents of mankind had lived in perfect harmony with nature, animate and inanimate. The Fall occurs in the world created by God for mankind at a time well after the Creation itself. But in Blake, the Creation and the Fall are the *same* event, a paradoxic state of affairs that offers still another key to Blakean symbolism. Such a view is scandalous to the literal or fundamentalist reader of Scripture, but given Blake's theory of the imagination, the paradox has a cogent, if poetic, logic: if the imagination is equally divine and human, then the Creation of man by God is a failure of the imagination, because such an act presupposes the separation of man and God. The banishment of man and woman from Paradise is but another version of what the orthodox account calls *creation*. The *Fall,* as a failure of the imagination, can only be reversed by an equally epoch-making act of the imagination, one that will put the fallen body of what Blake calls "the Human Image Divine" back together again. Such an act requires the destruction and transformation of the world as we know it, the events prefigured in the Revelation of Saint John the Divine. Genesis and Revelation, if read as allegories addressed to the intellectual powers, emerge as the two bookends of all we need know on earth, and the grand myth presented between those two texts provides the outline of virtually everything Blake has to say.

The metaphor of the Fall implies not only a story of change but a hierarchy of position, a spatial axis as well as a temporal one. From his survey of sacred and secular literature of the West, Frye discerns a shared mythological universe structured as four distinct levels of existence. These levels, at times only implicit or of marginal importance for some poets, are set out with great precision in Blake's work, though some of his names for the various states are idiosyncratic. Uppermost is a place Blake calls Eden, where creator and creature are one, where energy and form are united, a place more like a city than a garden.

Below it lies a land called Beulah (from the Hebrew for "married land") where lover and beloved are united with themselves, their offspring, and their world. Below these two states of the imagination is the world of Generation, that is, of ordinary experience as we know it. At the lowest reaches lies Ulro, the Blakean hell whose symbols are the rock and sand of infertility. It is peopled with brooding solitary subjects who stare out into space only to see their own image reflected back. Thus Ulro is single, Generation double, Beulah threefold, and Eden fourfold, the "fourfold vision" being the fullest, most imaginative model for poetic allegory. Even so comprehensive a vision as the Christian Trinity is thought inadequate because its fourth term is conspicuously absent.

In encountering the poetry of Blake for the first time, readers may well be confused by a puzzling set of values assigned to words and concepts whose positive character would seem assured. Terms like "angel," "prudence," and "moral virtue"— even "good"—are so imbued with a positive aura that their place in a hierarchy of values should be secure, almost by definition. But clearly a poet who could write "Sooner murder an infant in its cradle than nurse unacted desires"[17] goes a long way toward overturning conventional standards of ethics. Thus in his third chapter, which bears as its title the Nietzschean motto "Beyond Good and Evil," Frye takes pains to elucidate Blake's unorthodox lexicon of ethics and politics. He contends that Blake's political and ethical ideas are best understood in the light of his theory of knowledge, which holds that the imagination is the principle of action, and action the principle of life. Any reduction of imagination, Frye reasons, is thus a reduction of life itself, a sign of the "death-impulse." He can say, in paraphrasing Blake and following Milton, that "there can be no such thing, strictly speaking, as an evil act; all acts are good, and evil comes when activity is perverted into the frustration of activity, in oneself or others" (*FS,* 55). Given such a theory of action, it becomes clear why angels, as guardians against temptation, might be viewed negatively, or why the repressive mechanisms of what is called "moral virtue" are not in the least virtuous.

Political and ethical struggles are social in character and thus the focus of Blake's attention in this domain will be on the societal figure who best embodies the ideals of the imagination: the prophet. The Blakean imagination tends toward the apocalyptic, such that even mundane events of contemporary society can be viewed under the aspect of the Last Judgment. Blake's view of the prophet is a revisionary one. For him, the prophet is not typically the predictor of future events: "Prophets in the modern sense have never existed. . . . Every honest man is a Prophet."[18] The prophet is less the inspired figure who foresees future events than one who persuades his own contemporaries to follow a certain course of action.[19] He is, Frye notes, rarely caught up in a truly mass or popular movement himself, but nonetheless speaks as an iconoclast and revolutionary. The Hebrew prophet is the primary model for Blake here, but despite his disdain for Greek and Roman mythology, there is also much of the "modern Prometheus"—whose name means forethought—in Blake's prophetic figures.

Blake's time saw two "genuinely imaginative" upheavals in the American and French Revolutions, and he wrote poems—one of them called a prophecy—in sympathy with each revolution. But revolutions, as what Frye calls the "tragic irony" (*FS,* 218) of the word itself implies, tend to turn into their opposites in a seemingly endless cycle of power. This dynamic is illustrated in a number of poems that Frye christens "the Orc cycle," Orc being a young dynamo of political and sexual energy who confronts the aged and reactionary Urizen only to become in the end much like the opponent he tried to displace. Orc is for Blake the mythical embodiment of any number of revolutionaries whose historical failures have been manifested again and again. Thus Blake ultimately looks not so much to any one empirical model as an exemplary revolutionary, but rather to the biblical figure who is the beginning and end of all revolution, namely, Jesus. But why is it that Jesus—the divinely political model for Blake—becomes the cornerstone of the poet's *aesthetic?*

Art, in Frye's view of Blake, is the very form of religion, and the Bible is the single greatest "work of art." When Blake claims that the Old and New Testaments are the "Great Code of Art"—a phrase to be echoed in the title of Frye's magnum opus on the Bible—he means not only that it furnishes material for art, but that it is art in the first place. The Bible is a veritable compendium of literary genres, with Jesus' chosen mode of parable being but one among many others. For Blake, the Bible as a whole is one grand allegory, of which the life and teachings of Jesus form the central part. The Gospels are the key to the understanding of the Old Testament, and this structure of the Bible necessitates what might be called a "permanent revolution" in reading and rewriting. Frye notes that Jesus broke all of the Ten Commandments, "at least in theory," and in doing so he read the letter of the law (of what was quickly becoming the "Old" Testament) in a spiritual or allegorical way. "The letter killeth," said Saint Paul, and "the spirit giveth life." But the text of the New Testament becomes in its turn dead letters that must be given life. For Blake, the language of the Bible by no means exhausts the Word of God: the Word must be continually re-created and renewed.

In considering Blake as a "romantic" writer, one might assume that he would share certain fundamental tenets of what is often characterized as the romantic aesthetic, with its emphasis on the organic nature of art and the primacy of the ego or self as art's psychological foundation. Frye is careful, however, to distinguish Blake's position from that of his romantic contemporaries. Art for Blake is not mimetic of nature, as claimed in some branches of the Aristotelian tradition or more conspicuously in Coleridge, for whom *natura naturans* (nature in the process of growth) was the supreme model of art. Against the grain of romantic commonplaces about nature, Blake can write in *The Marriage of Heaven and Hell*: "Where man is not, nature is barren." Blake's paradigm for the aesthetic, in a further contrast to Coleridge and the dominant "myth" of romantic poetry, is not organic but mechanic: "Mechanical Excellence is the only vehicle of Genius." Blake may be the prophetic poet par excellence, but he places as much emphasis on craftsmanship and rhetorical exercise as he does on divine inspiration.

Although no art comes into being without the agency of an individual or group of individuals, the aesthetic work, for Frye, is not to be construed as the product of the artist's intention. The artist's conception, in effect, does not exist prior to the work itself but rather takes form in the execution. The implication for criticism is that reference to a poet's biography or psychology is unnecessary and indeed may prove an obstacle to the understanding of art. One might expect that in the case of lyric poetry some consideration of the poet was required, but even in the poetic mode that seems the most direct vehicle of self-expression, the critic's eye is properly focused on the text of the poetic "persona" and not on the author's personality.

Since poems, in Frye's view, come primarily from poems and not from "experience," the starting point for a discussion of Blake's canon is his relation to the literary tradition that precedes him. The most conspicuous fact of Blake's poetic thought is its massive debt to the Bible. And unlike poetic predecessors such as Milton and Spenser, Blake took the Bible as his model to the virtual exclusion of the mythology of Greece and Rome that informs so much of Western mythopoeic poetry.[20] At times, Blake's rewriting of the biblical myths seems

so eccentric as to constitute what has been called a "private symbolism." Blake's characters, for instance, bear such exotic names—Eni-
tharmon and Orc, Vala and Tharmas—that the reader is often at a loss
to relate them to anything recognizable in his or her literary experience. But Frye rejects the notion of a private symbolism and counsels
the reader to look past the characters' names to their characteristics,
and there one finds a nexus of symbols, images, and myths that derive
in large measure from the Bible.

Frye is interested not only in the myths that inform individual
poems of Blake but also in the plot of his career as a poet. The itinerary
of a poet's progress is a matter for much reflection and a good deal of
poetry from Virgil to Spenser and beyond. And indeed it is the shape
of the Blakean canon that lies behind Frye's choice of this poet as exemplary of "the poetic process." Blake begins his literary life with a
volume of poems entitled *Poetical Sketches,* a group of rhetorical exer-
cises including works such as "An Imitation of Spenser." The content
of these earliest poems is almost a matter of indifference, given the
nature of the task Blake set himself, but already one can glimpse the
outlines of a myth of tyranny and liberty that will structure Blake's
early prophetic poems, such as *The Marriage of Heaven and Hell, Europe,*
and *America.* Blake's poetic career moves from short lyrics (and failed
dramatic attempts) to short "prophecies"—an uneasy generic designa-
tion that applies to few other poems of Blake's time—and finally to
the epic prophecies *Milton* and *Jerusalem* that completed the canon.[21]
The move from lyric to epic was a gradual one: indeed, the shorter
prophecies such as *Europe* and *America* are on the border between lyric
and epic in many respects. And even the full-blown mythopoeic gran-
deur of *Jerusalem* does not preclude instensely lyrical moments that
recall his early sketches and songs.

Although we cannot follow him through all the labyrinthine details
of his unfolding of Blake's mythography, it is worth noting how Frye
seizes upon aspects of a single work that have more general, theoretical
consequences. Thus in his reading of Blake's *Milton,* Frye permits himself a number of seminal observations—indeed, theses—on the nature
of poetry and the function of criticism. *Milton* is unique among epic
poems in English because it takes a poet as its hero, which is one
indication of how lofty a conception Blake had of the poet's vocation.
This brief epic is a poem about "the self"—selfhood and self-sacrifice—
and the congruence of many of the details in the poem with certain
events in the life of Blake had led critics to view it as an intensely

autobiographical poem, a brief epic of "self-expression." But Frye uses the occasion of his commentary on *Milton* to point out the danger of confusing the poet's "life" with the poet's "imagination," the latter being the proper subject of Blake's poem. Frye cautions that "to dissolve art back into the artist's experience is like scraping the paint off a canvas in order to see what the real canvas looked like before it assumed its painted disguise" (*FS, 326*). In Frye's view, *Milton* is a poem not about the experience of a self but rather the "experience" of a literary tradition at a given moment.[22] In *Milton* Blake comes to terms with the tradition of biblical and Miltonic prophecy in preparation for writing the apocalyptic work in which his poetic career would culminate, namely, *Jerusalem,* a densely textured epic that rewrites British history from the standpoint of Revelation. Though Blake lived and worked for many years after finishing *Jerusalem,* that text nonetheless constitutes, for Frye, the completion of his poetic canon. Blake's subsequent production is either occasional poetry or not poetry at all, that is, visual art. It is no wonder that Frye's exemplary poet should "end" his career with a reworking of the end of the Bible, for *Jerusalem* constitutes the outer limits of what is possible for art within the tradition dominated by "the Great Code." Thus Blake's poetic production can be regarded as exemplary for its very itinerary, the "myth" or plot of the Blakean career, as it reinvents and parallels the movement of the Bible itself.

As Frye approaches the end of *Fearful Symmetry,* his own text takes on an increasingly apocalyptic tone. He widens his already considerable scope to address the questions of an all-encompassing generality with respect to literature and criticism. In his closing pages, Frye outlines the essential principles of criticism, all of which have been put into practice in the preceding commentary. "Every poet," he claims, "must first be studied in connection with his own age, but there comes a point at which the value of this study becomes exhausted and the conception of anachronism is rendered meaningless. What makes the poet worth studying at all is the ability to communicate beyond his context in time and space: we therefore are the present custodians of his meaning, and the profundity of his appeal is relative to our own outlook" (*FS, 420*). This is not at all to say the poet transcends his or her own time in all respects, a charge that is often leveled at Frye from critics of the Left. Marx himself was puzzled by the "eternal charm" of the Greek classics, which survive in societies radically different from the one in which they were produced. There is no doubt that Marx was conscious of the peculiar power of art—or rather of certain examples, and an unstable canon of them at that—to be in its effects trans-historical, if not transcendent. Frye will go well beyond his more historicist contemporaries to claim, by way of Blake, that "all symbolism in all art and all religion is mutually intelligible among all men, and that there is such a thing as an iconography of the imagination" (*FS*, 420). In keeping with his lament for the ignorance of allegory as a poetic mode, Frye proposes the Elizabethan mythographers as examplars of critical activity, for mythography is at once descriptive and interpretive, poised between literature and science. The task of the critic is simultaneously historical and rhetorical, diachronic and synchronic. The main focus for the archetypal critic is the structures of literary symbolism, but even the most elementary description of such structures must be informed by a sense of what Frye terms "the morphology of symbolism," the way images and archetypes are adopted and adapted over time. When reading a poet like Blake, one quickly becomes aware that literary history cannot be conceived as a provincial or national affair but rather that it entails, in the West, a good deal of the Judaeo-Christian tradition: the classics of Greece and Rome (even if they function primarily as negative examples for Blake), as well as the less familiar body of Oriental and Nordic myths. The synthetic activity of Blake's imagination, in which almost anything is identifiable with anything else, leads Frye to postulate a "grammar" of iconography potentially available to any poet. Frye uses the figure of grammar advisedly because he is referring to the underlying structure and discursive preconditions of any poetic text. In linguistics, the seventeenth-century myth of a universal grammar has largely faded away, but is is less easy to dismiss such a notion with respect to the grammar of literature, especially if "grammar" not be understood in unduly narrow fashion. No literary text is reducible to its grammar—Frye would never claim that it was—but the text is always a necessary function of it. Poetic grammar, in the sense of an underlying structure of myth and symbol, is simply the privileged object of study for the archetypal or anagogic critic.

Frye's text ends, one could say, at its beginning, for it culminates in a pronouncement of "first" principles, the rudiments for any systematic study of literature. It is this very movement back to basics that prepares the way for the apocalyptic closing, though it is an apocalypse qualified by a note of irony. The closing sentences take the reader to the "gates" of Blake's vision. "But gates," Frye says, "are to be opened,

and there is still much to be seen by the light of the vision Blake saw—
perhaps the same light that broke in on the dying Falstaff when he
babbled of green fields and played with flowers, and on his hostess
when she told how he had gone into 'Arthur's' bosom, and how he had
talked of the Whore of Babylon" (*FS*, 428). In ending where Blake,
Falstaff, and his hostess do, Frye aligns his own vision with theirs, but
not without a certain critical distance. Still, it is no accident that the
text concludes with a visionary passage from Shakespeare that passes
easily from Arthurian romance to the Book of Revelation. Indeed, it is
the one goal of Frye's criticism to be able to account for and to perform
such movements. I have alluded to the epic structure of *Fearful Symmetry*, and epic is one of the few genres capable of including apocalypse
within its margins. Frye's next major work would take the anatomy as
its generic model, another genre so comprehensive that it too can en-
compass apocalypse. *Fearful Symmetry* had tested a hypothesis on the
workings of "the poetic process," but had confined itself to Blake and
the tradition of visionary, mythopoeic poetry. Still much concerned
with allegory and the mechanisms of myth, Frye would now in the
Anatomy of Criticism widen his horizons to test the power of criticism
to develop a language adequate to nothing less than the whole of Western literature.

Chapter Two
Anatomy as Criticism

Anatomy of Criticism is arguably the most important work of literary theory of this century. No other text of its kind rivals it in comprehensiveness: its dazzling scope alone guaranteed it a place at the center of critical debate. Its center lies in the Anglo-American tradition, but its appeal has been worldwide, having been translated into eight languages. And not only did the *Anatomy* touch on all the critical issues of literary theory—thus making it of potential interest to virtually every teacher, scholar, and critic of literature—it was executed with such wit and clarity that it became a touchstone text for readers from the most advanced of theorists to the newest students of literature. Its project is ambitious in the extreme, nothing less than to provide a synoptic view of everything that criticism does and should do, a task which in turn would entail an inductive survey of the "whole" of literature. Frye somehow managed to survey that immense field of world literature and criticism with a degree of profundity not approached by his contemporaries and hardly by any of his predecessors. Though several claims of the *Anatomy* cannot and have not gone unchallenged, its reader is nonetheless left with the impression that Frye has attained a singular authority by virtue of his immense reading and analytical acumen; his voice, at times, seems to speak from the standpoint of literary tradition itself.

The *Anatomy* is avowedly an attempt to consider literature as a whole in the light of principles formulated in Frye's study of Blake. The project began as a study of Spenser's *The Faerie Queene,* but soon became enmeshed in a labyrinth of theoretical and terminological problems, such that the book resulted in a work of metacriticism.[1] Most works of theoretical criticism argue for a single position and against a number of others, but the task Frye sets himself is virtually unique, in that the four "essays" of the *Anatomy* attempt a synoptic view of criticism as a whole. The "whole" of criticism is addressed in theoretical terms rather than, say, historical ones: the *Anatomy* is by no means a chronological survey of what criticism has done from Aristotle to Arnold and beyond.

The most striking aspect of the *Anatomy* is its "scientific" or systematic character, its contribution of a conceptual framework for literary criticism. Frye's proposal is for something of a "new science," for he finds the state of literary criticism in conceptual disarray, not even having the proper words, much less the proper concepts, to address the central issues involved in the understanding of literature. The "scientist," according to one view of science, should speak a "universal language," and his or her scientific claims are supposed to be true to the extent that they are universal. But what Frye finds to be universally true has by no means been universally acknowledged as such, and so at the outset he has to part company from many of his fellow literary critics in a "Polemical Introduction."

Polemics

By criticism, Frye means "the whole work of scholarship and taste concerned with literature" (*AC*, 3), an activity he finds an essential aspect of liberal education and, indeed, of culture generally. In order to clear the way for his plea for the importance of criticism, Frye must first dispel a certain number of myths circulating in criticism's name: for example, that the critic is a failed or frustrated artist whose work is "parasitic" on true art. Not only is this psychologizing of the critic irrelevant, it fails to realize first, that criticism, like its subject matter, is "something of an art" and, second, that art demands criticism because criticism can talk but the arts are "dumb." Works of art, even those consisting only of words, cannot "speak" of what they are. They invite and even demand criticism of some sort, though not necessarily of an academic or scholarly kind. This is true enough simply in conceptual terms, but Frye adds the compelling point that a culture thrives on the memory of itself, and without criticism culture would be in danger of losing its memory.

Frye's most encompassing thesis, of which the entire text is a vast illustration, is that "criticism is a structure of thought and knowledge existing in its own right, with some measure of independence from the art it deals with" (*AC*, 5). This is not at all to suggest that criticism is an isolated activity of ivory-tower academics, as several critics of Frye have charged, but simply to contend that criticism has a specific conceptual framework that cannot be subsumed either by art or by any other intellectual discipline. Similarly, when Frye claims that "poetry

is a *disinterested* use of words: it does not address the reader directly"
(*AC*, 4), he by no means suggests that poetry is not caught up in a
social and economic network of interests.[2]

When Frye describes criticism as "a structure of thought and knowledge," the phrase is distinctly analytic: what is usually called "art appreciation" is the furthest thing from Frye's mind. Blake, we recall,
defined the most sublime poetry as allegory addressed to the *intellectual*
powers. Not that art has nothing to do with emotion or feeling, but
these sentiments (in the artist, the work, or the reader) are only of
interest insofar as they contribute to the comprehension of art. There
is no room in the anatomy lesson of Dr. Frye for those who feel of
poetry that "we murder to dissect."

As a rule, the focus of a literary critic will be the explication of a
single text (or several related ones) from a single, given perspective
that promises to be illuminating. The *Anatomy* is an attempt to account
for all the possible and desirable acts of criticism and Frye contends
that criticism "has to be based on the whole of what literature actually
does" (*AC*, 7). The whole of what literature actually does is distinct
from what many authors and critics have claimed for it. A common
fallacy Frye finds operative is the device of putting one's "favorite study
into a causal relationship with whatever interests [one] less" (*AC*, 6).
To succumb to this tendency is, in Frye's view, to abandon the specific
conceptual framework demanded by literature and to assimilate criticism to some extracritical system, be it psychological, sociological, or
otherwise: "The first thing the literary critic has to do is to read literature, to make an inductive survey of his own field and let his critical
principles shape themselves solely out of his knowledge of that field.
Critical principles cannot be taken ready-made from theology, philosophy, politics, science, or any combination of these" (*AC*, 6–7). The
word "inductive," as Frye notes, suggests some sort of scientific procedure. By "science" Frye means any coherent body of knowledge and
he invites the reader to substitute the word "systematic" or "progressive," if the connotations of "scientific" seem unsuitable. Clearly, literary criticism is not an exact or pure science: Frye's *Anatomy*, as its
title suggests, is poised halfway between clinical procedure and literary
genre, and as such is emblematic of the status of criticism in general.[3]

Frye's claim that "it should be possible to get a comprehensive view
of what [criticism] is actually doing," echoes his earlier contention that
criticism should attend to what "the whole of literature actually does."
But whereas the critic must be as catholic as possible in his or her

acceptance of literature, there is no such necessity with respect to the whole of criticism. There is much that Frye finds lacking in what passes under the name of criticism, some of which he can even term "meaningless." For the most part, these forms of pseudocriticism involve a move away from the text or literature as a whole to some supposedly surer ground from which literature can be understood and evaluated.

The most fundamental principles of literary criticism, according to Frye, should be readily intelligible: indeed, one should be able to write an "elementary textbook" containing them. That Frye chooses this figurative scheme to discuss the topic is one illustration of his desire to "democratize" criticism, an endeavor that, in practice, often risks being arcane and overspecialized.[4] An initial task for the author of such a textbook is to outline the primary categories of literature, based again on an inductive survey of the whole of literature. Frye finds to his dismay—though convenient for his own project—that "the critical theory of genres is stuck precisely where Aristotle left it" (*AC*, 13). And since Aristotle could not have been conversant with the numerous genres and subgenres that have flourished since his time, there is much inductive study that has to be accounted for by a "theory of criticism," which is what Frye says Aristotle meant by "poetics."

I noted with regard to *Fearful Symmetry* that Frye's working hypothesis was the total coherence of Blake's work; at the outset of the *Anatomy,* Frye assumes nothing less for the whole of literature. This gesture Frye calls an "inductive leap," that is, a jump from the mere aggregate of readings of individual works of literature to the general view of literature's coherence. The coherence in question is not provided by "tradition" (which is really based on a notion of chronology in disguise), though it does involve the relation of literature to primitive culture. An inductive survey of literature reveals it to be a series of complications "of a relatively restricted and simple group of formulas" (*AC*, 17). Paradoxically (for some), it is in the great masterpieces of literature that these "primitive" formulae surface again and again. This claim is easily demonstrable and no one has defended it more successfully than Frye. But the hypothesis that follows is more dubious. Noting that the study of mediocre works is "a random and peripheral experience" whereas the real masterpiece seems to contain an "enormous number of converging patterns of significance," Frye goes on to wonder "if we cannot see literature, not only as complicating itself in time, but as spread out in conceptual space from some kind of center that criticism could locate" (AC, 17). The figure of the "center" is crucial and characteristic for Frye: it organizes many schemas throughout the *Anatomy* and elsewhere. But the "center" is by no means necessary even for a scientific or systematic criticism such as Frye proposes. Indeed, structuralist thought from Saussure onward has demonstrated that the units of systems need only be differentiated from each other, without requiring a single center around which all else would turn.[5] Whether Frye's center can "hold" or not remains to be seen in the course of the *Anatomy*. Initially, though, Frye gives some idea of what the center of literature might be, namely what he calls "the order of words," analogous to the "order of nature" that is the basis for the intelligibility of the natural sciences. But why an "order of words" in the singular? Does the fact that the great masterpieces of literature rework primitive formulae mean that literature as a whole is homogenous enough to be addressed in such terms? It is here in the positing of a center for literature and literary criticism that Frye is seduced by what might be called the schematic imperative. The value of some of Frye's practical schemas is apparent to many readers, but that practical insight cannot simply be translated back into the conceptual principle of a centered literary universe.

But if one grants the hypothesis of a center for literary criticism grounded in the order of words, the task then is to distinguish between what does and what does not contribute to systematic criticism. And here we arrive at the crucial meditation on the role of evaluation in criticism, a subject on which Frye has been much misunderstood. A good deal of what has passed for criticism should more precisely be called "taste," and Frye observes that the history of taste "is no more a part of the *structure* of criticism than the Huxley-Wilberforce debate is a part of the structure of biological science" (AC, 18). There is no denying that value judgments play a considerable role in critical activity, but that does not imply that criticism as knowledge should be confused with value judgments informed by taste. As Frye observes: "Shakespeare, we say, was one of a group of English dramatists working around 1600, and also one of the great poets of the world. The first part of this is a statement of fact, the second a value-judgment so generally accepted as to pass for a statement of fact. But it is not a statement of fact. It remains a value-judgment, and not a shred of systematic evidence can ever be attached to it" (AC, 20). René Wellek, one of the most eminent of literary historians of the twentieth century, thinks he has found something contradictory in Frye when in the same work the latter can denounce value judgments and yet describe *The Birds* as Aristophanes' "greatest" play or Burton's *Anatomy of Melancholy* as "the greatest Menippean satire in English before Swift."[6] The point is, however, that not all statements made by critics are of the same order of criticism. The ranking of poets may be a pleasant pastime or even a practical, pedagogical necessity, but such activities do not contribute to the analytic and descriptive project of systematic criticism. On inspection, most "critical" value judgments turn out to be projections of social judgments, often more concerned with the anxieties of the writer and the reader than with rhetorical or structural analysis. But if a principle of value derived from something other than the literary field is enlisted in a critical program, then the tendency will be to "reject half the facts of literary experience" as a whole. The critic must try, by a certain imaginative effort, to "look at art from the standpoint of an ideally classless society" (*AC*, 22).[7]

The "Polemical Introduction" closes with a confession that it was "written in the first person plural, and is quite as much a confession as a polemic" (*AC*, 29). The views expressed, then, are necessarily those of the author, but they are of interest to Frye only insofar as they contribute to the advancement of theoretical and practical criticism. In his apologia, Frye declines to apologize for the schematic character of the book, though he attaches no importance to the schematism itself, describing it as mere scaffolding "to be knocked away when the building is in better shape" (*AC*, 29).

Historical Modes

At the beginning and end of *Fearful Symmetry* Frye contended that criticism of Blake should start out with a consideration of him in his historical context, and the *Anatomy,* in somewhat similar fashion, begins with "Historical Criticism: A Theory of Modes." In the reception of Frye, this chapter has received far less attention than the subsequent two on "Symbols" and "Myths," the concerns that are more closely associated with his most distinctive contributions to criticism.[8] But the historical survey proposed in the opening essay is clearly germane to the entire project, for even if the ultimate aim is to establish a typology of archetypes and symbols, Frye must first account for the almost bewildering variety of works encountered in any inductive survey of the whole of literature.

Taking his cue from a remark in Aristotle's *Poetics* to the effect that fictions can be differentiated by the "elevation" of the characters in them, Frye in this first essay proposes to classify all fictions according to the hero's power of action, "which may be greater than ours, less, or roughly the same" (*AC*, 33). This produces a schema of five categories: myth, romance, high mimetic, low mimetic, and irony. The terms will be crucial for the text as a whole and so it will be helpful here to quote Frye's distinctions at length:

1. If superior in *kind* to other men and to the environment of other men, the hero is a divine being, and the story about him will be a *myth* in the common sense of a story about a god. Such stories have an important place in literature, but are as a rule found outside the normal literary categories.
2. If superior in *degree* to other men and to his environment, the hero is the typical hero of *romance*, whose actions are marvelous but who is himself identified as a human being. The hero of romance moves in a world in which the ordinary laws of nature are suspended. . . . Here we have moved from myth, properly so called, into legend, folk tale, *maerchen*, and their literary affiliates and derivatives.
3. If superior in degree to other men but not to his natural environment, the hero is a leader. He has authority, passions, and powers of expression far greater than ours, but what he does is subject both to social criticism and to the order of nature. This is the hero of the *high mimetic* mode, of most epic and tragedy, and is primarily the kind of hero that Aristotle had in mind.
4. If superior neither to other men nor his environment, the hero is one of us: we respond to a sense of his common humanity, and demand from the poet the same canons of probability that we find in our own experience. This gives us the hero of the *low mimetic* mode, of most comedy and of realistic fiction. . . .
5. If inferior in power or intelligence to ourselves, so that we have the sense of looking down on a scene of bondage, frustration, or absurdity, the hero belongs to the *ironic* mode. This is still true when the reader feels that he is or might be in the same situation, as the situation is being judged by the norms of a greater freedom.

(*AC*, 33–34)

This abstract, seemingly atemporal scheme suddenly assumes a historical character when Frye notes that "the center of gravity" tends to move downward on the list as one follows the lines of literary history. Thus myth predominates in biblical and classical literature, romance in the medieval period, high mimetic in the Renaissance, low mimetic in the eighteenth and nineteenth centuries, and irony in our own century. Frye by no means suggests that there is no romance, say, in the nineteenth century; his general scheme is just that, general. It stands or falls on its ability to characterize broad cultural patterns, not all possible examples and counter-examples.

The five modes are also historically marked by whether they are "naive" or "sentimental," terms Frye borrows from Schiller. The sentimental, or what in Schiller could be liked to the self-conscious, is for Frye "a later recreation of an earlier mode" (*AC*, 35), as the artistic fairy tale is, in large measure, a re-creation of the popular folktale. The modes are also inflected in yet another way, depending on whether the hero is isolated from or incorporated into society, the former being tragic and the latter comic.

Thus a fictional work can be classified in a preliminary way as belonging to one of the five modes of myth, romance, high mimetic, low mimetic, or irony, at the same time that it is either tragic or comic, as well as naive or sentimental. This permits, in theory, many combinations and permutations, and the fact that Frye does not pursue all the "possibilities" has been offered as evidence that this schema is not "logical."[9] What critics of Frye fail to realize is that the "logic" of literature is derived after the fact, from an inductive survey of literature. So that if, say, high mimetic comedy does not correspond to high mimetic tragedy in the excellence of its examples or in the counterpoint of its characteristics, it is through no fault of Frye's. The question is whether the schema is appropriate to the evidence of literature, not how symmetrical or "logical" the schema is in itself.

We cannot pursue Frye though all the details of the exposition in the first essay, in which he traces each of the five fictional modes in their broad historical movements and each mode as it is variously inflected as tragic or comic, naive or sentimental. The latter categories are not explicitly invoked at every possible place on the grid, although Robert Denham, in opposition to some of Frye's hasty critics, has shown that the examples given are rather exhaustive even in this regard.[10] For practical criticism, a principal effect of showing the sequential movement of the modes is the necessity for "a more flexible meaning to some of our literary terms" (*AC*, 49). For example, the terms "romantic" and "realistic" emerge as absolutely relative. As Frye observes: "If we take the sequence *De Raptu Prosperpine, The Man of Law's Tale, Much Ado about Nothing, Pride and Prejudice, An American Tragedy*, it is clear that each work is "romantic" compared to its successors and "realistic" when compared to its predecessors" (*AC*, 49). Moreover, literary modes such as "realism" and "naturalism" now emerge not so much as purely descriptive and referential as one phase among other conventions whose claim to imitation of nature is complicated precisely by its status as convention. The principal insight that emerges from Frye's survey of the modes of fiction in their sequence is that the later mode tends to be a *displaced* version of the earlier. That is to say, "myths of gods merge into legends of heroes; legends of heroes merge into plots of tragedies and comedies; plots of tragedies and comedies merge into plots of more or less realistic fiction" (*AC,* 51).[11] Imitation of nature, then, produces "not truth or reality, but plausibility," and canons of plausibility vary substantially from one historical moment to the next.

Although Frye provisionally treats each of the five major modes as distinct, he contends that "once we have learned to distinguish the modes . . . we must then learn to recombine them" (*AC,* 50). Indeed, though each work tends to have an underlying tonality, there is nothing to prevent the simultaneous co-presence of every mode: some works even thrive on a certain modal counterpoint, as does Joyce's *Ulysses.* Moreover, the flexibility of Frye's categories derives in part from their status as both historical and systematic.[12] Thus there is a period—the Middle Ages—when romance is so dominant a mode as to be characteristic of the entire era, and yet romance is equally a mode that can unite writers of utterly diverse eras, from Homer to William Morris and beyond.

The historical criticism of modes is further divided into two categories, fictional and thematic, with both terms being used in somewhat unconventional senses. For Frye, fiction is literature in which there are internal characters, whereas in thematic literature the principal relation is between the author and his audience, writer and reader. The former category, as we saw, includes such forms as the epic, the drama, the romance, and the novel. Frye groups the lyric and the essay among the thematic modes, where the character is the author or a certain persona addressing a real or imagined audience. Some genres such as parable and allegory can be located in either fictional or thematic modes, depending on the degree to which the internal characters are prominent or secondary. The distinction between fictional and thematic remains somewhat arbitrary because every work, regardless of its genre, has at once a fictional and a thematic aspect.

Thematic modes, like fictional ones, move through phases that are broadly though not entirely chronological in sequence. Thus the lyric and the epic, or what Frye prefers in this context to call the "episodic" and the "encyclopedic," are distinct when "modulated" by the five modes of myth, romance, high mimetic, low mimetic, and irony. As an exemplary paradigm of such a modal morphology, Frye singles out the figure of the poet as it is variously conceived in history. In the mythical mode, the legendary poet is a spokesman for the gods and virtually indistinguishable from them. In the mode of romance, the god has retreated to the sky and the poet is fully human, though he continues to sing to and of his nation from memory, a memory that is inspired by the gods who only recently left. The high mimetic poet is a courtier, preacher, or orator, and the theater of the world becomes the dominant fictional medium in which he works. The typical low mimetic poet is the "romantic," the latter term now being used in its more historically circumscribed sense. Here the poet is still an extraordinary figure, whose imagination allows him or her to rise above nature, but the world confronted is that of ordinary experience, the world, say, of Wordsworth's *Lyrical Ballads*. Finally, one arrives at the ironic mode of the symbolist writers, Mallarmé, Rilke, Eliot, and Joyce, in whom there is as much myth as irony, thus marking a turn back to the beginning of the cycle.[13]

Frye's task in outlining the course of thematic modes throughout literary history is primarily descriptive. But the inductive survey leads to several critical principles, the foremost of which is that "no one set of critical standards derived from only one mode can ever assimilate the whole truth about poetry" (*AC*, 62). Frye himself has been charged with promoting romance to such an extent that his view of literature as a whole is skewed, but it remains to be seen whether the primacy of romance in Frye is "theoretical" or "practical," an essential aspect of his vision, a mere accident of taste, or a polemically strategic position.[14]

Symbols

Having established a framework for the historical understanding of literature in the opening essay, Frye turns next to a subject closer to the center of poetics, namely, an analysis of the literary symbol. Frye entitles the second essay "Ethical Criticism: Theory of Symbols," using the term "ethical" in somewhat idiosyncratic fashion, since ethos for him refers to the "internal social context of a literary work" (*AC*, 365). Moreover, Frye's initial definition of symbol is so general as to promise little illumination, since the symbol is "any unit of any literary structure that can be isolated for critical attention" (AC, 71). But Frye's definition at this point must be comprehensive enough to include what he will outline as the four fundamental aspects of the literary symbol: as sign (or motif), image, archetype, and monad.

Frye proceeds on the assumption of the doctrine—most commonly associated with the medieval theory of fourfold allegorical meaning— of literature's "polysemous meaning."[15] If multiplicity of meaning is inscribed into the literary text, it is no wonder that a number of different critical methodologies will develop to account for the multifaceted phenomenon that is literature. But polysemous meaning does not lead simply to a pluralism of critical method. We should consider the possibility, Frye contends, "that there is a finite number of valid critical methods, and that they can all be contained in a single theory" (AC, 72).

The many aspects of the literary symbol are divided by Frye into four phases, the most elementary of which is the symbol as sign or motif. The verbal symbol as a sign represents something other than what it is, that is, the black marks on a white page that say "cat" can be understood as standing for an actual cat or more likely, the idea of a cat.[16] The reading of a symbol as a sign entails an outward or centrifugal movement of the mind. But literary symbols do not exist by themselves: they always form part of a sequence or structure and as such they are motifs, the recognizable verbal elements or units of any given work.

Although the reading process will always entail both centrifugal and centripetal movements, Frye proposes that literary verbal structures can be classified according to whether the final direction of meaning is inward or outward. In literature proper, that direction is ultimately inward, since literary works do not primarily describe or assert: they are neither true nor false but rather "hypothetical" or "imaginative." As Frye says: "the poet, like the pure mathematician, depends, not on descriptive truth, but on conformity to his hypothetical postulates" (AC, 76).[17] The postulates of literature turn out, on inspection, to be highly conventionalized, and the understanding of literature depends to a considerable degree on the informed acceptance of the postulates of literary convention.

The simplest kind of descriptive or representational meaning Frye calls literal. Understanding a poem literally means "understanding the whole of it, as a poem, and as it stands. Such understanding begins in a complete surrender of the mind and senses to the impact of the work as a whole, and proceeds through the effort to unite the symbols toward a simultaneous perception of the unity of the structure" (*AC*, 77).[18] The comprehensive account of the literary work will consider the movement of the work as well as its structure, its mythos as well as its "dianoia," Aristotle's word for thought, idea, or theme. The notion of "simultaneous perception" may sound like a rather mystical formulation, but it refers to the process of abstraction that is a necessary component of any act of comprehension. As Frye says: "When we think of a poem's narrative as a description of events, we no longer think of the narrative as literally embracing every word and letter. We rather think of a sequence of gross events, of the obvious and externally striking elements in the word-order" (*AC*, 78–79). Thus even the most elementary understanding of a literary work will begin to turn the text into something other than what it says, which is why one can say that in general the literary structure is ironic: "'what it says' is always different in kind or degree from 'what it means'" (*AC*, 81).[19]

To this point in the essay on "Ethical Criticism," Frye has been considering literature almost as if it were an instance of language in general, leaving aside aesthetic considerations. The most striking characteristics of literary language, however, derive from its formal properties, and so Frye turns next to the formal phase of symbolism, where the symbol is no longer a mere sign but an image. Form is the shaping or containing principle of literature and the materials it works with may be called images, as distinct from the concepts of philosophy or the events of history. And formal criticism, in Frye's account—which is part descriptive and part prescriptive—"begins with an examination of the imagery of a poem, with a view to bringing out its distinctive pattern" (*AC*, 85). Formalist criticism is commentary that turns the imagery of a poem into discursive propositions; thus all commentary is allegorical interpretation, whether or not the object of interpretation is itself a formal allegory. Commentary differs as texts range from naive or explicit allegory—where the direction of commentary is prescribed by the text—to the paradoxical and hermetic rhetoric of the symbolist poets, which seems by design to resist the translation proper to interpretation. Although I cannot recapitulate here Frye's survey of the whole spectrum of such texts, it is worth noting one of its achievements, that being the recognition that literature is a body of hypothetical creations, "which is not necessarily involved in the worlds of truth and fact, nor necessarily withdrawn from them, but which may enter into any kind of relationship to them, ranging from the most to the least explicit" (*AC*, 92–93). Thus the relation of literature to life is "potential." At its best, art exemplifies what Blake claimed for it in the aphorism "exuberance is beauty." The literary work of art, then, should be the liberating force at the center of a "liberal" education.[20]

An inductive survey of literature shows that poems are not only imitations of nature or action as Aristotle had set out in the *Poetics*, but also that poems are to a considerable degree imitations of other poems. As Frye says in a stark formulation that aroused much criticism: "Poetry can only be made out of other poems; novels out of other novels" (*AC*, 97). This would seem to beg the question of how the first poems or novels could be written but Frye's main point is well-taken. There are no such things in nature as the shaping principles of literature, to say nothing of literary forms such as the sonnet. The sonnet is a highly conventionalized literary genre that does not correspond to anything outside of language. The most striking fact derived from a survey of world literature is the tenacity of what Frye calls, in a provocative metaphor, the "communism of convention" (*AC*, 98), the great body of structures, plots, and motifs that cannot be the property of any single author.

Attention to the markedly conventionalized texture of literary forms shows that the symbolism of poetry, considered (from something of a remove) as a technique of civilization, organizes itself in terms of archetypes. Archetypes, most often natural objects endowed with human meaning, are recurring symbols that form associative clusters. There are no necessary correspondences between the archetype and what it comes to represent: it is, in Carlyle's terms, an extrinsic rather than an intrinsic symbol. Moreover, archetypes, though drawn from the natural world, are not simply representative of it; Frye claims that the significant content of archetypal criticism is: the "conflict of desire and ritual which has for its basis the work of the dream" (*AC*, 105). Archetypes, according to Frye, are best studied in highly conventional literature. And, as it happens, the greatest works of literature tend to be precisely those of an archetypal character.[21] In speaking of archetypes, Frye has recourse again to a rhetoric of "centrality," but that figure, whose problematic character I noted above, will be considerably qualified in the final section on the anagogic phase of symbolism.

The archetypal critic looks at literature as a product of civilization and its objects of study are typically primitive and popular, using these two terms in their nonpejorative senses. The elements of such literature—the recurrent images of the city, the garden, the sea—stand up under the pressure of considerable translation over time and space. In the vision of human work constructed from archetypal symbols, some aspects of civilization are highly valued and others neglected. And thus the social context of art is necessarily a moral one as well. But here one must be careful not to bring back the specter of evaluation that was chased out in the "Polemical Introduction." Art may always be value-laden, but Frye notes with approval that it is "an elementary axiom in criticism that morally the lion lies down with the lamb" (*AC,* 114). The critic must, at one level, be able to accept the likes of a Marquis de Sade as well as a Jane Austen. Otherwise literary criticism would be little more than a vehicle for thinly veiled moralizing.

The literary work of art is necessarily social and moral, but that is not to say that the poet should strive for or can achieve some combination of the true, the beautiful, and the good—an alliance the German critic Walter Benjamin termed "the bourgeois trinity." Indeed, the deliberate, direct pursuit of beauty, truth, or goodness detracts from the poet's task *qua* poet. The poet works best by what the prosaic Polonius calls "indirections." The work of art is valuable not so much for what it describes but for its potential relation to reality. The imagination then is, when considered as a function of human desire, a liberating force, whatever the character of its changing contents. The archetypal vision is one of the total form of human civilization, but even this is not the conceptual, or better the mythopoeic, limit of literature. Beyond the archetype lies the ultimate horizon of the anagogic.

Anagogic is a term taken from the medieval doctrine of the four levels of meaning, in which it occupies the highest position of all. It is redefined by Frye as "relating to the total order of words," and typically the anagogic phase includes the most encompassing of fictions relating to divine or quasi-divine beings. In commenting on this phase of symbolism which marks the limit of the human imagination, Frye's own rhetoric is heightened almost to the point of a religious experience:

In the greatest moments of Dante and Shakespeare, in, say, *The Tempest* or the climax of the *Purgatorio,* we have a feeling of converging significance, the feeling that here we are close to seeing what our whole literary experience has been about, the feeling that we have moved into the still center of the order of words. Criticism as knowledge, the criticism which is compelled to keep on talking about the subject, recognizes the fact there *is* a center of the order of words.

(AC, 117–18)

This exalted "feeling" that Frye posits as universal for all readers quickly turns into an argument about the nature of literature and the scientific status of criticism: "Unless there is such a center, there is nothing to prevent the analogies supplied by convention and genre from being an endless series of free associations, perhaps suggestive, perhaps even tantalizing, but never creating a real structure" (AC, 118). I alluded above to the general insight of certain structuralist and poststructuralist thinkers that a system need not be organized around a center, and it is precisely in the case of language, Frye's "order of words," that no stable center can be found.[22] Frye's claim here for a "still center" detracts, unnecessarily, from his outline of the structure of symbolism. Despite the resolute formulation of the necessity for such a center, however, Frye goes on only a few pages later to say that "the center of the literary universe is whatever poem we happen to be reading" (AC, 121). The still center, then, cannot quite hold; at the very least, it is always on the move. The metaphor of the center loses much of its conceptual force when any text and any reader can be located as the center(s) of the literary universe. But even in its qualified form the figure retains something of a theological aura, for even God has been described as a center that is everywhere and nowhere.

The texts of the anagogic phase of symbolism, such as the epics of Dante and Milton, move in the spheres of the eternal, the infinite, and the apocalyptic, offering analogues to scriptural revelation. Some critics of Frye see his emphasis on these texts as part of an attempt to present literature as religion in disguise, but Frye, as a literary critic, is only interested in religion as the content of poetry.[23] Frye says that even "the loftiest religion, no less than the grossest superstition, comes to the poet, *qua* poet, only as the spirits came to Yeats, to give him metaphors for poetry" (AC, 125). Religion, then, is only privileged for literary reasons, insofar as its discourse is one of infinite action and infinite thought that represent the limits of the human imagination. At the outer limit of the anagogic vision we have the mind of a universal man speaking a universal creative word. Frye remarks: "About this man and word we can, speaking as critics, say only one thing ontologically: we have no reason to suppose either that they exist or that they do not exist. We can call them divine if by divine we mean the unlimited or projected human" (*AC*, 125). One implication of this passage—which is much informed by Blake's revisionary Christianity—is that the anagogic is the phase of symbolism that operates par excellence in the mode of the supposition or the hypothetical. If the anagogic receives a certain prominence in Frye, it is not because it is religious but rather because it best exemplifies the hypothetical character of literature as a whole.

Myths

With the third essay, "Archetypal Criticism: Theory of Myths," the reader arrives at what is often regarded as the central achievement of Frye's work. This essay is not only the longest of the book, it is the one in which Frye's erudition seems most productively applied. This essay is also the most relentlessly schematic of the four, not unlike Yeats's *A Vision* with its system of elaborate, counterpointed phases.[24] The first task of the essay is to sketch the structures of literary imagery at the level of the archetype. "Imagery" suggests an analogy to painting and the visual arts, but Frye cautions against taking this analogy too far. The theory and practice of painting have been dominated by a tendency toward representation, which in literature translates as "lifelikeness." Frye has already begun to show how lifelikeness (or verisimilitude) plays a relatively minor role in Western literature, much more of a special case than the paradigm for literature as a whole. Music offers a better parallel for literature, since it is nonrepresentational (or nonobjective, as Frye prefers to say): its notes do not refer to anything other than themselves, and so its formal properties are all the more open for inspection.

Frye's overarching purpose in the third essay is to "outline a few of the grammatical rudiments of literary expression" (*AC*, 133). The forms of literary expression are limited in number and scope, such that it should be possible to formalize these rudiments. To recognize these elements of literature it is necessary to "stand back" from the details of the literary text, and here Frye has recourse to an analogy with painting, not for its representational character but for the more fundamental element of design. The passage, which has received much commentary and criticism, merits quotation in full:

In looking at a picture, we may stand close to it and analyze the details of brush work and palette knife. This corresponds roughly to the rhetorical anal-

ysis of the new critics in literature. At a little distance back, the design comes
into clearer view, and we study rather the content represented: this is the best
distance for realistic Dutch pictures, for example, where we are in a sense
reading the picture. At a great distance from, say, a Madonna, we can see
nothing but the archetype of a Madonna, a large centripetal blue mass with a
contrasting point of interest at its center. In the criticism of literature, too,
we have to "stand back" from the poem to see its archetypal organization. If
we "stand back" from Spenser's *Mutabilitie Cantoes*, we see a background of
ordered circular light and a sinister black mass thrusting up into the lower
foreground—much the same archetypal shape we see in the opening of the
Book of Job. If we "stand back" from the beginning of the fifth act of *Hamlet*,
we see a grave opening on the stage, the hero, his enemy, and the heroine
descending into it, followed by a fatal struggle in the upper world. If we
"stand back" from a realistic novel such as Tolstoy's *Resurrection* or Zola's *Ger-
minal*, we can see the mythopoeic designs indicated by those titles.

(*AC*, 140)

William Wimsatt, in his feisty response to Frye, objects to the stance
necessary for the archetypal view by asking simply: "Who really wants
to see a painting that way?"[25] If that were the only way Frye advocated
looking at a painting, or a literary work of art, then there might be
something gravely wrong with his view. But Frye explicitly proposes
a whole range of things to do with a poem, only one of which is to
"stand back" to afford a view like that offered of *Hamlet*. No criticism
could limit itself to such statements because at such a level of archetypal abstraction there are severely limited things that one could say
about any given text.

   The stance of the distanced observer applies as much to literary history as to the individual text, and Frye's survey from such a vantage
point produces a schema still more abstract than that of the five modes
discerned in the first essay. For the present context, Frye sees literature
moving in a sequence of three phases: myth, romance, and realism
(myth being understood here in its purest or "undisplaced" form). The
imagery of myth is the starting point for an understanding of literature
because it is there that archetypes are most clearly spelled out. And
Frye begins a discussion of archetypal meaning by focusing on apocalyptic literature precisely for the clarity with which it reveals its own
schemes. The end point of the Bible then becomes the starting point
of analysis, because the Book of Revelation constitutes a veritable
"grammar of apocalyptic imagery" (*AC*, 141).

   Apocalypse is perhaps the most extreme form that the archetypal imagination can assume. What eighteenth-century aestheticians would call the "faculty" of imagination works on the givens of the material world (animal, vegetable, and mineral) and produces, most typically, the sheep, the garden, and the city as its archetypes. Each of these is, in the metaphoric logic of apocalypse and of poetry generally, identifiable with any of the others. These identifications, moreover, can be extended to the human and divine spheres, so the Bible, for example, can equate—and the mathematical metaphor is appropriate for this level of abstraction—the one God with the one man with the one lamb with the one tree (of Life) with the one building or temple. These metaphorical schemes are by no means limited to the highly figurative texts of the Bible or of poetry generally. Frye's example of the primacy of corporeal metaphors in political philosophy from Plato to Hobbes and beyond is only one among many possible choices.[26]

In direct opposition to the apocalyptic symbolism lies the "presentation of the world that desire totally rejects" (*AC*, 147), the world we call demonic. If the divine world of apocalyptic imagery resembles heaven, then the demonic divine world works, so to speak, like hell. The demonic too has its gods but they are the distant sky-gods who seem to embody a blind and cruel fate. Its human representatives range from tyrants to sacrificial victims. This world is inhabited not by apocalyptic sheep but by demonic wolves; the demonic desert replaces the apocalyptic garden, and so forth. The way these images function in literature has little or nothing to do with how these animals behave in real life. The signs of literary language have no necessary or natural relation to what they signify: a tree is not in itself demonic or apocalyptic, but at times there could hardly be more at stake for the reader, as once for Adam and Eve, than in distinguishing one tree from the other.

The demonic and apocalyptic represent the outer limits of the imagination; much of literature moves in the middle ground between those two extremes. This region would contain the high mimetic, low mimetic, and romance, but Frye reduces the three categories to the two more general ones of "romance" and "realism." This permits a Blakean distinction between innocence and experience to structure the middling ground of literature, with the idealizing mode of romance constructed according to the "analogy of innocence" and realism to the "analogy of experience." Analogy here is the structural term that marks what in the first essay was called displacement, the revision of an earlier mode in the direction of greater plausibility. If metaphor is the characteristic trope of the apocalyptic and demonic, simile is the more appropriate figure for romance and realism.

The structure of imagery can only be abstracted from a reading of a text through time but that structure, which Frye identifies as "the meaning of a poem" (AC, 158), is itself a static pattern. This sounds to some of Frye's critics, especially certain leftists committed to the idea of dialectical change, as if Frye is being reductively spatial, atemporal, and ahistorical. But structure is not, for Frye, a category opposed to movement. Indeed, one must consider the structure of imagery and *mythos* (plot, narrative) as equally constitutive of a poem. The two fundamental movements of narrative, according to Frye, are the cyclical and the dialectical, the former moving "within the order of nature" and the latter moving "from that order into the apocalyptic world above" (AC, 161–62). The movements take place within two spheres, one of romance and one of realism, the former organized by the analogy of innocence and the latter by the analogy of experience: "There are thus four main types of mythical movement. The downward movement is the tragic movement, the wheel of fortune falling from innocence toward hamartia, and from hamartia to catastrophe. The upward movement is the comic movement, from threatening complications to a happy ending and a general assumption of post-dated innocence in which everyone lives happily ever after" (AC, 162). The four movements may be termed romantic, tragic, comic, and satiric or ironic, categories that are more encompassing than, or logically prior to, the ordinary literary genres. To each mythos Frye assigns a season: thus comedy is called the mythos of spring, romance the mythos of summer, tragedy the mythos of autumn, and the ironic or satiric, the mythos of winter. The alignment of myths with seasons suggests that their movement is cyclical at the same time that it marks a certain characteristic mood or tonality. It of course does not mean that all tragedies take place in winter, and William Wimsatt's objection that the Greeks did not know the four seasons as we do—but only two—is a merely pedantic objection that misses its target.[27]

Of the four mythoi, comedy seems perhaps the most "tenacious of its structural principles." Both the movement and the characters of comedy are remarkably consistent from Aristophanes and Plautus to Shaw and Chaplin. Frye draws most of his examples from dramatic comedy but it is important to recognize that the comic is not confined to the drama. Many of the same principles will hold for the "comic" novels of Fielding as well as they do for plays. Greek New Comedy, which has come down to us through its reception in Plautus and in Terence, is, in Frye's view, "less a form than a formula" (*AC*, 163). The typical plot can be easily summarized: "What normally happens is that a young man wants a young woman, that his desire is resisted by some opposition, usually paternal, and that near the end of the play some twist in the plot enables the hero to have his will" (*AC*, 163). The fate of the hero and heroine is usually bound up with some larger movement from one kind of society to another, often marked by a wedding, dance, or festival that includes as many of the play's characters as possible. Following a tradition that dates back to the *Tractatus Coislinianus*, Frye likens the movement of comedy to the action of a lawsuit "in which plaintiff and defendant construct different versions of the same situation, one finally being judged as real and the other as illusory" (*AC*, 166). Shakespearean comedy in particular features numerous examples of a comic action that "begins with some absurd or irrational law" that will be overruled, as it were, in the end.[28]

The drive toward a "happy ending" is pervasive in comedy, so much so that the plot tends to overwhelm its characters. Character then becomes more clearly a function of plot than in more realistic modes of fiction. The plot of comedy can sustain seemingly inexplicable changes of heart and mind, a cruel governor or parent can relent at the last minute and the quadruple weddings of a Shakespearean comedy can be based on the principle that Walter Benjamin in another context called "love at last sight." Any attempt to study the characters of comedy in purely psychological terms will be doomed to misunderstanding.

Within the same general structure of comedy, the emphasis can fall either on the blocking characters or on the forces of reconciliation: the former is the tendency of comic irony, satire, and realism and the latter the tendency of romantic comedy. Indeed, the nominal or "technical" heroes and heroines may be of very little interest as characters but they are indispensable for the comic *mythos*. The characters who take the center stage of our interest are often excessive or absurd, dominated by a "humor" or ruling passion. Frye catalogues the main types of comic character: the *alazon* or impostor, the *eiron* or self-deprecator, the buffoon, and the *agriokos*, that is, a person who is churlish or rustic. Again, these are not characters who correspond very closely to actual people. The "representation" of life is sacrificed to the presentation of plot.

The comic structure is capable of containing a wide range of moods from "savage irony to the most dreamy wish-fulfillment" (*AC*, 177).

To account for this diversity within the overarching pattern, Frye adopts the figure of "phases": "I recognize six phases of each *mythos*, three being parallel to the phases of the neighbouring *mythos*. The first three phases of comedy are parallel to the first three phases of irony and satire, and the second three to the second three of romance. The distinction between an ironic comedy and a comic satire, or between a romantic comedy and a comic romance, is tenuous, but not quite a distinction without a difference (*AC,* 177). The determination of six phases for each of the four *mythoi* has seemed unduly diagrammatic for many of Frye's critics, but the symmetry of his categories should not be exaggerated. Not all the phases of comedy feature similar examples, either in strength or number. Not all of them are homogenous enough even to be assigned a name.

The most ironic phase of comedy is the first, in which a "humourous society triumphs or remains undefeated," as in Ben Jonson's *The Alchemist*. In the second phase, the hero escapes or runs away from a society rather than transforming it. The third phase of comedy is the most typical one—already outlined—in which an angry, paternal figure blocks the erotic desires of a young man and woman. These first three phases are contained by the world of experience, whereas the last three operate in the idealized world of innocence and romance. The fourth phase of comedy is typified by Shakespeare's romantic comedies, in which the action takes place on two levels of society at once. The beginning and end of such comedies will resemble those of the first three phases, the difference being that much of the central action takes place in what Shakespeare calls the "green world," a realm of magic and fantasy, or natural supernaturalism. Frye describes the fifth phase of comedy as a "world still more romantic, less Utopian and more Arcadian, less festive and more pensive" (*AC,* 184). These five phases of comedy constitute not only a typology but something of a "sequence" as well. They

may be seen as a sequence of stages in the life of a redeemed society. Purely ironic comedy exhibits this society in its infancy, swaddled and smothered by the society it should replace. Quixotic comedy exhibits it in its adolescence, still too ignorant of the ways of the world to impose itself. In the third phase it comes to maturity and triumphs; in the fourth it is already mature and established. In the fifth it is part of a settled order which has been there from the beginning, an order which takes on an increasingly religious cast and seems to be drawing away from human experience altogether.

(*AC,* 185)

The final phase of comedy presents the collapse and disintegration of comic society, marked by a primacy of small groups or individuals. It is the world of "ghost stories, thrillers, and Gothic romances." The sixth is the "final" phase of comedy because it corresponds, in the sequence of the life of a redeemed society, to the moment of death.

Clearly such distinctions depend on questions of nuance and nicety, so that no summary can do what Frye does best: persuade the reader by the range and the acuity of his references and allusions. Some critics have been suspicious of the cyclical or circular character of Frye's phases, as if the figure of the circle were vaguely religious or mystical. But the circle or cycle suggests itself as a figure for the phases because the beginning and end of each phase cross over into one another. Frye's schematizations simply mark, after the fact, the possible forms a genre can take. The assignation of a certain play to a certain phase of comedy has little to do with the interpretation of that play as such: the point of the schemas is to shed some light on the "grammatical" possibilities of genre.

If comedy is the mythos of spring, romance as the mythos of summer cannot be far behind.[29] Frye shows how the comedies of Shakespeare already possessed a strong romantic element, with their central action set in a "green world" of dreams, magic, and intrigue. This fourth phase of comedy gave way to a fifth, more properly romantic phase, which includes the "romances" of Shakespeare such as *Pericles* and *The Winter's Tale*. But romance, within the genre of comedy, is more a matter of setting than structure. As Frye says of romance proper: "The essential element of plot in romance is adventure, which means that romance is naturally a sequential and processional form, hence we know it better from fiction than from drama" (*AC,* 186). The sequence tends to unfold in three movements: the *agon* or conflict, the *pathos* or death-struggle, and the *anagnorisis,* or discovery, in which the hero is recognized as a hero. In part because the emphasis in romance is on sequence, characters tend to be rather one-sided. The structure of romance is dialectical, which demands stark oppositions between characters rather than the subtleties appropriate to, say, the psychological novel. In his purest—which is perhaps also his most extreme—form, the romantic hero is rather like the Messiah, a deliverer or redeemer who comes from an upper world to defeat the demons and dragons of the demonic, lower world. And indeed for Frye, the Bible is, among other things, the great paradigm of romance, even more so than Homer's *Odyssey*. Though the Bible ultimately has the structure of a (divine) comedy, it encompasses a whole series of romances and romantic heroes from Moses to Joshua to Jesus. The Bible in turn becomes the model for many of the great romances of English literature, the most notable example being Book I of Spenser's *The Faerie Queene*, which might be described as a rematch of the *agon* from the Book of Revelation.

Romance, too, is divided into six phases, and like comedy, they form a sequence modelled on the rhythm of life, this time not of society as a whole but of the individual protagonist. The first phase is the "myth of the birth of the hero," the mysterious birth being a hallmark of romance narrative that will survive to a remarkable extent in the eighteenth and nineteenth century novel. The second phase features the "innocent youth of the hero," for which the archetypes are Adam and Eve before the Fall. The third phase, as in comedy, is the most typical one of quest romance outlined above. The principal theme of the fourth phase is the maintenance of the integrity of the "innocent world against the assault of experience" (*AC,* 201). Like the fifth phase of comedy, the corresponding one of romance is reflective and idyllic, presenting a view of experience from the perspective of a higher world. The sixth phase of romance is marked, like its comic counterpart, by the disintegration of society into small groups or individuals, like the hermit or solitary. As the sequence progresses, Frye's figurative scheme of charting the phases of romance against the phases of the hero's life drops out, though it is easy to see how the figure of the elder or sage would fit with the final phases of romance.

Frye shares something of the mania that drove Milton to do every-thing himself, but even so he is grateful to find that the study of tragedy, the mythos of autumn, is in considerably better shape than the other *mythoi,* thanks to Aristotle's *Poetics.* (Frye spends much less time on the shape, characters, and phases of tragedy than on any other *mythos.*) What sets tragedy apart is the "disinterested" quality it guar-antees, quite unlike the make-believe realms of comedy and romance. Tragedy focuses on the individual and however great, noble, or quasi-divine the hero or heroine is, he or she is subject to the constraints of natural and often supernatural law. Whereas the movement of comedy goes against the grain of absurd or irrational law, tragedy often cul-minates precisely in "an epiphany of law, of that which is and must be" (*AC,* 208). Tragedy eludes reduction to simplistic formulae about the omnipotence of fate or the "tragic flaw," the dubious translation of Aristotle's *hamartia.* In its movement beyond good and evil tragedy forces a critical movement beyond mere thematic considerations toward a recognition of something like a structural imperative.

Coming as it does between romance and irony, the first three phases of tragedy correspond to the first three of romance, and the last three to the last three of irony. The parallels are not exact, as is clear from Frye's description of the first phase, "in which the central character is given the greatest possible dignity in contrast to the other characters" (*AC*, 219). Though Frye aligns this phase with the myth of the birth of the hero in romance, he admits that the alignment must be somewhat skewed, given the "unusual difficulty of making an interesting dramatic character out of an infant" (*AC*, 219). Frye posits that the corresponding central figure of this phase is the calumniated woman, such as the heroine of *The Duchess of Malfi*. Thus the parallel exists only at a considerable degree of abstraction where one can locate a common trait such as possession of "the greatest possible dignity." In the second phase, corresponding to the youth of the romantic hero, the parallels are more readily available: one can point to the examples of Romeo and Juliet or Iphigenia as young heroes and heroines whose lives are "tragically" cut short. Tragedy's third phase corresponds to the typical romantic quest, with the emphasis on the hero's achievement. The typical fall of the hero though hubris (which is not simply overweening pride but also violence or aggression) and hamartia constitutes the fourth, most common phase of tragedy. The fifth phase moves increasingly toward irony, as the hero, like Shakespeare's Timon of Athens, appears in a smaller perspective. The extremes of the tragic vision are reached in the sixth phase, "a world of shock and horror in which the central images are images of *sparagmos*, that is, cannibalism, mutilation, and torture" (*AC*, 222). A play like the *Oedipus Tyrannus* straddles the borderline between the fifth and sixth phases, given its simultaneous emphasis on the diminution of the hero (through his lack of knowledge) and the sheer horror his actions provoke.

At the end of Frye's natural cycle comes the mythos of winter: irony and satire. The twin focus of this mythos causes a shift in the presentation of the argument: Frye eschews giving first a general outline of the myth, followed by a sketch of the characterization appropriate to it. Instead Frye begins immediately with his outline of the six phases, the first three of the order of satire and the last three of irony. The two terms are distinct but related, for satire, according to Frye, is "militant irony." Irony is so elusive a mode that it is often difficult to detect, whereas the position of satire is more pointed and palpable, a kind of flagrant excess being one of its distinguishing features. "Satire," says Frye, "is irony which is structurally close to the comic: the comic struggle of two societies, one normal and the other absurd, is reflected in its double focus of morality and fantasy. Irony with little satire is the non-heroic residue of tragedy, centering on a theme of puzzled defeat" (*AC*, 224).

The first phase of satire corresponds to that of ironic comedy, in which there is no displacement of the humorous society. The world of absurdity and injustice is simply taken for granted: Frye calls this the satire of the low norm. What tends to be satirized in this phase is the unconventional: the prophet, the saint, or the crackpot with a new theory, even if that theory will turn out in the future to be true. The next phase passes to satire of "the sources and values of conventions themselves," and here one finds a version of phase-two comedy, the comedy of escape. This takes the form, in satire, of the picaresque novel, with the iconoclastic rogue as its hero. This quixotic phase of satire often takes as its theme "the setting of ideas and generalizations and theories and dogmas over against the life they are supposed to explain" (*AC*, 230). The third phase of satire, that of the "high norm," is characterized by a certain disintegration, when even common sense has to be abandoned as a standard. Frye's examples for the various phases of satire seem to lead in many directions, exceeding the limits of his definitions. No doubt this is in part because satire is notoriously hybrid: "the word satire is said to come from *satura*, or hash, and a kind of parody of form seems to run all through its tradition, from the mixing of prose and verse in early satire to the jerky cinematic changes of scene in Rabelais" (*AC*, 233–34).

In passing from the third to the fourth phase, one moves from satire to the ironic aspect of tragedy, in which tragedy is seen "from below, from the moral and realistic perspective of the state of experience" (*AC*, 237). In this phase of irony, the action is very much like tragedy, the difference being that it appears comprehensible or intelligible. Here the sense of inevitable fall is minimized but the fifth-phase of irony emphasizes the relentless turn of the wheel of fortune, the unending cycle of nature. At the outer limits of irony is the representation of life "in terms of largely unrelieved bondage" (*AC*, 238). This is the world of Orwell's *Nineteen Eighty-Four* or the novels of Kafka, a world of dungeons and prisons, pain and death. With this phase Frye has reached the end of his survey of myths, but he is almost constitutionally incapable of ending an essay on a bleak note and so he ends with citing the example of Dante's journey through hell, which involves climbing around the loins of Satan to regain a view of the universe. Frye comments: "From this point of view, the devil is no longer upright, but standing on his head, in the same attitude in which he was hurled downward from heaven upon the other side of the earth. Tragedy and tragic irony take us into a hell of narrowing circles and culminate in some such vision of the source of all evil in a personal form. Tragedy can take us no farther; but if we persevere with the *mythos* of irony and satire, we shall pass a dead center, and finally see the gentlemanly Prince of Darkness bottom side up" (*AC*, 239).

Rhetoric

Some readers never make it past the third and longest of the essays in the *Anatomy*, the essay, moreover, which is taken to be the most characteristic of Frye's work. The fourth essay, "Rhetorical Criticism: Theory of Genres," then, is somewhat neglected in the reception of Frye's work, though its inclusion as the final essay adds an important perspective to the scope of Frye's criticism. Not only is the focus on rhetoric important in its own right, it also anticipates much of what has proved valuable in the literary criticism of the three decades since the *Anatomy*.

It should come as no surprise that Frye's book ends in the "center," that is, the place from which literature emanates. Following a time-honored tradition from Plato to Poe, Frye locates literature and art in the middle of a tripartite scheme. To one side lies the world of social action and events, on the other lies the sphere of individual thought and ideas. Literature then occupies a middle ground between history on the one hand, philosophy and science on the other. Similarly, the poetic symbol is portrayed as "intermediate between event and idea, example and precept, ritual and dream" (*AC*, 243). The fourth essay treats literature in its aspect of rhetoric, and rhetoric in its turn appears in another tripartite scheme, the trivium of liberal arts consisting of grammar, rhetoric, and logic. Frye notes that "there is a sense—a literal sense—in which grammar and narrative are the same thing; as logic may be called the art of producing meaning, there is a sense in which logic and meaning are the same thing" (*AC*, 244). Where then does rhetoric fit in? "Rhetoric," says Frye,

has from the beginning meant two things: ornamental speech and persuasive speech. These two things seem psychologically opposed to each other, as the desire to ornament is essentially disinterested, and the desire to persuade essentially the reverse. In fact ornamental rhetoric is inseparable from literature

itself, or what we have called the hypothetical verbal structure which exists
for its own sake. Persuasive rhetoric is applied literature, or the use of literary
art of reinforce the power of judgment.

(AC, 245)

Frye's attention to the doubleness of rhetoric, as ornament and persuasion, goes against the grain of much literary criticism, for which rhetoric was becoming increasingly a matter of ornament, where the
emphasis was on tropes and figures rather than persuasion.[30] Though
persuasion is not the essence of literature, the presence of it—and the
presence of tropes and figures in "nonliterary" discourse—guarantees
that the differences between discourses are ones of emphasis not essence. In general, nonliterary discourse aims at describing states of
affairs and thus seeks a "direct union of grammar and logic." Literature, on the other hand, "may be described as the rhetorical organization of grammar and logic" (AC, 245). And rhetoric here must be
understood to include both ornament and persuasion.

Until this point in the *Anatomy*, Frye has been concerned primarily
with questions of literary structure, but rhetoric, especially in the
mode of persuasion, raises the specter of a reader or an audience. The
traditional tripartite division of genres into epic, lyric, and dramatic
presupposes differences in what Frye calls "the radical of presentation."
(By "radical" here Frye means the structure or inherent constitution of
the literary genres.) "Words," he says, "may be acted in front of a
spectator; they may be spoken in front of a listener; they may be sung
or chanted; or they may be written for a reader" (AC, 247). The basis
for criticism according to genre, then, is rhetorical, organized in terms
of the relations between the poet and the public. The radicals of presentation are not always distinct, even for the same text. A play of
Shakespeare may be read in a book as well as acted on the stage, but
Frye says that in any case "the purpose of criticism by genres is not so
much to classify as to clarify . . . traditions and affinities, thereby
bringing out a number of relationships that would not be noticed so
long as there were no context established for them" (AC, 247–48).

To the division of three genres handed down to us from the Greeks
Frye adds the fourth of fiction, an omission for which Aristotle may be
forgiven. Each genre, broadly conceived, has for Frye a distinctive
rhythm. By the term "epos" Frye does not mean epic in its ordinary
generic sense but rather "extended poetry in meter." Thus the ballads
of Burns and Coleridge fall under this category as much as the epics of

Homer and Virgil. The distinguishing characteristic of epos is a regular pulsating meter, an intensified version of the "rhythm of recurrence," recurrence being a structural principle of all art. Although this principle suggests analogies with music, Frye resists the maudlin or "sentimental fashion of calling any poetry musical if it sounds nice" (*AC,* 255). Actual music is constructed along the lines of tension and a driving accented impetus whereas what is called musical in poetry is usually a balancing of vowels and consonants as well as a "dreamy sensuous flow of sound," which is not for Frye musical in any technical sense.[31]

Following the lead of Aristotle's *Poetics* by situating the *lexis* or rhetoric of poetry between *melos* (rhythm, sound) and *opsis* (spectacle), Frye turns from the musical to the visual aspect of poetry, but he may be following the Aristotelean schema somewhat grudgingly here. He is able to demonstrate some remarkable visual effects but one gets the sense that, unlike *melos, opsis* is more a special case than an essential aspect of poetry. This is entirely consistent with Frye's tendency to think of literature as nonrepresentational or nonobjective. There is something irreducibly verbal about language, such that, when applied to literature, critical terms like imagery and vision are always themselves metaphorical.

Prose has a different principle of organization from the recurrence of epos. Continuity characterizes the rhythm of prose, a fact "symbolized by the purely mechanical breaking of prose lines on a printed page" (*AC,* 263). Not having the preestablished pulsating meters of epos, prose resorts to various devices such as antithesis and alliteration in the rhetorical deployment of both ornament and persuasion. In prose style, the exploitation of *melos* and *opsis* is relatively rare. What really characterizes prose style, for Frye, is "the conception of the sentence" (*AC,* 267).

In turning to drama, Frye must come up with a corresponding "rhythm," which proves much more difficult in this instance. Frye rightly draws attention to the structure of dialogue that sets drama apart from other genres and notes that the principal stylistic problem of drama is "the suiting of style to an internal character or subject." Decorum is the appropriate term for this relation of style to content, but can one really speak of drama in terms of "the rhythm of decorum"? Is decorum of the same order as recurrence or continuity such that one could consider them under the single rubric of "rhythm"? Frye does succeed in showing how the figure of stichomythia, a trading of lines like something of a verbal fencing match, is appropriate to drama's tendency to express both the rhythm of speech and the character's "character," so to speak. Still it is noteworthy that Frye can only devote two pages to the rhythm of decorum as opposed to a dozen on the rhythm of epos. Decorum emerges as something of a pseudorhythm, when compared to recurrence and continuity, but at least Frye does not distort the facts of dramatic literature to make them correspond to the other major genres.

Frye is much more expansive when he comes to lyric, the final of the four genres, which he discusses as the rhythm of association. He is of course on surer ground in speaking of various sorts of rhythm in the lyric. The hallmark of lyric, especially in relation to prose, is its discontinuity. The typical rhythm of lyric is described as "oracular," which in a example from Shakespeare is linked with other predicates like meditative, irregular, and unpredictable. Much of poetic creation, in Frye's view, comes from beneath the threshold of consciousness, where a number of associative rhetorical procedures take priority over logical sense or assertive truth. Simply in a formal way, the lyric is discontinuous, constructed as it is in stanzas with lines that do not usually stretch to the margin of the page.

In his treatment of lyric Frye passes almost imperceptibly from "association" at the level of rhetoric and form to association at the thematic level by noting that "the traditional associations of lyric are chiefly with music" (AC, 273). Again, one must be careful not to press the analogies between music and poetry too far. Frye proposes to translate the catchphrase of Greek aesthetics *ta mele* as "poems to be chanted," and he goes on to observe that "Modern poets who, like Yeats, want their poems chanted are often precisely those who are most suspicious of musical settings" (AC, 273). If *melos* represents one tendency of lyric, the other is in the direction of *opsis*. The extreme form of lyric *opsis* would be the emblematic poems, such as some of Herbert's, the shapes of which mime their content.

The lyric often represents itself as proceeding from the unconscious or the threshold between consciousness and the unconscious, and this "fact" has implications for the tendency of lyric toward *melos* and *opsis*. Frye proposes, in a gesture that mocks the poverty of critical vocabulary at the same time that it demystifies critical jargon, to call the unconscious drives toward *melos* and *opsis* "babble" and "doodle." "Babble" denotes the verbal wordplay of puns, assonance, alliteration, and even rhyme, whereas "doodle" stands for rough sketches of verbal design, the elementary tendency toward the diagrammatic that organizes so much literature (to say nothing of the *Anatomy of Criticism*). But Frye's playfulness with terms gives way to more sober academic rhetoric, and he eventually replaces babble and doodle by charm and riddle, respectively.[32] The riddle seems exemplary for lyric because it entails "a fusion of sensation and reflection, the use of an object of sense experience to stimulate a mental activity in connection with it" (*AC,* 280). This fusion of abstract and concrete, characteristic of all art, is brought to the foreground in the highly metaphorical language of the lyric, metaphor being the only way possible to bridge the abstract and concrete.[33] The lyric at its most distinctive goes "beyond" metaphor and is characterized by catachresis, which Frye glosses as the "unexpected or violent metaphor" and which most rhetoricians define as an abuse of words.

One consequence of Frye's insistence on considering *lexis* or verbal pattern in relation to *melos* and *opsis* is the necessity of rethinking traditional categories of genre. The distinction between tragedy and comedy, for example, is fine as far as it goes, but it cannot account for a dramatic form like the masque. The same holds true for the medieval mystery play and other examples of dramatic spectacle. Frye proceeds to catalog a whole series of "specific forms," dramatic, thematic (encompassing lyric and epos), and prose fiction, charting the principal features of what are now often called subgenres. We need not pursue the specifics of Frye's catalog but one genre invites particular attention, since it is the form of Frye's own text. One of Frye's most constant polemical targets is the false primacy of the novel as a paradigm for fiction as a whole and sometimes even for literature in general. And in the fourth essay, the most impressive section is that which outlines the many faces of prose fiction and thus demonstrates that the novel is but one among other forms with rich and somewhat autonomous traditions of their own. Frye observes the considerable difficulty many critics, much less nonprofessional readers, would have in classifying certain prose fictions. *Gulliver's Travels* seems quite distinct from the novel that came to be codified in Swift's century and the next, but what exactly is it? Frye proposes the term "Menippean satire" to name the genre that includes Swift's *Gulliver,* Rousseau's *Emile,* and Huxley's *Brave New World.* In contrast to the novel's representation of characters involved in a series of actions, the Menippean satire presents "mental attitudes." Moreover, at its most concentrated it offers "a vision of the world in terms of a single intellectual pattern" (*AC,* 310). With this

phrase the reader may well begin to think that Frye includes his own
text in this genre. And indeed Frye shortly turns to consider a neglected subspecies of Menippean satire, namely, the anatomy. "The
Menippean satirist dealing with intellectual themes and attitudes,"
Frye observes, "shows his exuberance in intellectual ways, by piling up
an enormous amount of erudition about his theme . . ." (AC, 311).
The anatomy is one form that the tendency toward the encyclopedic
takes, "dissecting" or analyzing everything in its path. Though anatomy is introduced as one subspecies of Menippean satire, Frye's special
interest in the form is clear when he proposes to replace the older, more
cumbersome term by the newer, and seemingly more specific one. The
definition of anatomy is a pivotal passage because it marks the moment
when the text, in purely structural terms, reflects upon itself and the
consequences of the moment are crucial for an understanding of Frye's
project. Frye had claimed in his "Polemical Introduction" that criticism was in part a literary art and he specifies that his own chosen
genre is a species of fictional satire. Thus Frye calls attention to the
way his own anatomy is a fictional undertaking as well as a scientific
one. One consequence of this reflection on the fictional status of the
anatomy is a certain qualification of the claim to scientificity. To a
considerable extent, Frye acknowledges, in an ironic or understated
fashion, his imposition of a single, vast intellectual pattern on the
chaotic variety of the literary world.[34]

The final section of the fourth essay, where Frye takes up the question of "The Rhetoric of Non-literary Prose," also reflects back on the
text of the *Anatomy*. At the outset of the chapter Frye had remarked
on the traditional division of rhetoric into the two functions of ornament and persuasion. Non-literary prose, which does not share precisely the same status of the hypothetical verbal structure that poetry
or fiction does, aims at persuasion more resolutely than literature does.
And in doing so it will not stoop to make use of all the ornament it
can muster for the cause of persuasion. Nonliterary prose, as Frye noted
earlier, aims at the coincidence of logic and meaning but the only road
from grammar to logic "runs through the intermediate territory of
rhetoric" (AC, 331).

In summarizing this phase of his argument Frye says the essay: "led
to the principle that all structures in words are partly rhetorical, and
hence literary, and that the notion of a scientific or philosophical verbal
structure free of rhetorical elements is an illusion. If so, then our literary universe has expanded into a verbal universe, and no aesthetic
principle of self-containment will work" (AC, 350). This would seem

a simple point, and, indeed, by now Frye's argument has become some-thing of a critical truism: who would not agree with Frye's claim that "the nature and conditions of *ratio,* so far as *ratio* is verbal, are con-tained by *oratio*" (*AC,* 337), which is to say that any "rational" argu-ment is inscribed in a certain rhetorical scene of persuasion?[35] Yet a prominent critic in a highly regarded book, Frank Lentricchia in *After the New Criticism,* can introduce the passage just quoted in this way: "in Frye's book we see the entire neo-Kantian aestheticist movement brought to its logical conclusion: from the holistic holiness of the sin-gle poem, to the privileging of the entire canon of all literary objects as the literary universe, to the highest of all aestheticism (the term now becomes meaningless) in which every act of making is glorified as art."[36] The errors here, many of them symptomatic, are numerous and egregious. The least important of these is the muddled logic by which Lentricchia complains that to conceive of the entire canon of literary objects as the literary universe is somehow an act of "privileging." But Lentricchia's misreading continues to more serious problems. In the passage in question, Frye claims that nonliterary prose is "partly rhe-torical and hence literary," that is, it has tropes and figures, as well as rhetorical strategies of presentation and persuasion in common with literary texts. Frye by no means turns all of science and philosophy into art, much less does he make all art the object of "aestheticism." It is clear from Frye's study of Blake onward that he has little ideological sympathy with "art for art's sake" in the reductive, "decadent" sense of the phrase. Lentricchia's misreading of Frye, which forces him to say exactly the opposite of what the text says, is in turn based on a mis-reading of Kant's aesthetics. For Kant, art was indeed determined as "purposiveness without purpose," but at the same time the aesthetic was conceived as the bridge between pure reason and practical reason, between thought and action. Lentricchia must first reverse what Frye explicitly says about the impossibility of a principal of aesthetic self-containment before he can proceed to criticize the simulacrum he cre-ated in the first place. If nothing else, however, Lentricchia demon-strates the necessity of reading nonliterary prose, including Frye's, with attention to its rhetoric.

The End of Criticism

Frye calls the final section of the *Anatomy* the "Tentative Conclusion," but more than one commentator has noted that the tone is by no means tentative as he proceeds rather from the Olympian perspective that he attains through the cumulative achievement of the first four essays. However, the word "tentative" here retains its Latin sense of something "to be attempted": Frye ends by setting out his program for literary criticism as a whole in the light of his inductive survey of literature as well as his theoretical meditations on the conceptual framework required for its "scientific" study. Frye's most distinctive contribution consists in archetypal or myth criticism, but it is crucial to recognize that Frye calls for a comprehensive criticism that includes the formalist, the historian, New critics and old. Frye's polemical intent is to bring archetypal criticism to the point where it supplements allegorical criticism, a term that includes virtually every sort of commentary.

Frye recalls his argument of the "Polemical Introduction" that the arts do not progress, but he adds quickly that there is nothing to prevent the comprehension of art from progressing. The understanding of art has a twin historical focus: on the moment of a work's production and the moment of its reception. A literary work will always be inscribed in a historical moment, and Frye observes that if "we cut through history at any point, including our own, and study a cross-section of it, we get a class structure" (AC, 346). But the ultimate aim of art for Frye, following Matthew Arnold, is the withering away of the class structure. A principal function of liberal education is to make inroads, however modest, toward that goal. The goal is clearly utopian but that is precisely what makes the production and understanding of imaginative literature a more pressing concern than might be thought. Frye has been taken to task for his claim that "the imaginative element in art . . . lifts [works of art] clear of the bondage of history" (AC, 347). The objections have come largely from Marxist critics who misconstrue Frye's statement to be ahistorical, but Frye's emphasis is on "bondage" not "history."[37] And indeed Frye's Blakean view of the liberating function of the work of art is compatible in some respects with much of Marxist aesthetics, such as those of Herbert Marcuse and Ernst Bloch.[38] For Frye there is no question of lapsing into mere formalism or aestheticism: "no discussion of beauty can confine itself to the formal relations of the isolated work of art; it must consider, too, the participation of the work of art in the vision of the goal of social effort, the idea of a complete and classless civilization" (AC, 348). Thus the work of art is not simply the object of aesthetic contemplation but "an ethical instrument" as well. Frye would be the first to concede that such a program for criticism, with its ultimate goal of a classless society, is patently utopian. But in searching for the nowhere that is literally utopia, one is more likely to end up somewhere than if one abandoned the search in the first place.

In closing, Frye returns again to the analogy between literature and mathematics, with their common basis in the hypothetical postulate as their paradigmatic form. As languages, literature and mathematics represent no truths in themselves though they "provide the means for expressing any number of them" (*AC,* 354). Together they point to a higher intellectual universe than the objective world as understood by common sense. This higher world can never quite be reached, and thus story of the Tower of Babel comes back to haunt criticism. But the ultimate goal of criticism as Frye envisions it is an attempt to restore the lost unity, of whose fragmentation the plurality of languages is one sign. In the final paragraph Frye goes beyond the dispassionate, disinterested tone of the "anatomy" to interpret a dream in what is itself a kind of reverie:

> If I have read the last chapter of *Finnegans Wake* correctly, what happens there is the dreamer, after spending the night in communion with a vast body of metaphorical identifications, wakens and goes about his business forgetting the dream, like Nebuchadnezzar, failing to see, or even to realize that he can use, the "keys to dreamland." What he fails to do is therefore left for the reader to do, the "ideal reader suffering from the ideal insomnia," as Joyce calls him, in other words the critic. Some such activity as this of reforging the broken links between creation and knowledge, art and science, myth and concept, is what I envisage for criticism.
>
> (*AC,* 354)

In a gesture rather like the ending of *Fearful Symmetry,* Frye assumes a prophetic posture that claims much for the future of criticism. Criticism must pick up where literature itself leaves off, and, after having gone through the painstaking dissection of the body of world literature, it has to put the pieces of literature—and much more—back together again. Frye speaks of this future as if it will certainly come to pass, whether or not critics consciously attempt to bring it about. And, indeed, a good deal of criticism in the "wake" of the *Anatomy* has gone about the interpretation of Frye's dream.

Chapter Three
The Romance of Romance

At the beginning of *A Natural Perspective,* a study of Shakespearean comedy and romance, Frye remarks on the habit of mind that tends to divide whole realms of experience in two, as Coleridge divided all philosophers into Platonists and Aristotelians. Frye proceeds in similar fashion to divide all literary critics into *Iliad* and *Odyssey* critics, those whose visions find their center in tragedy and realism or comedy and romance, respectively. Well aware that they are a much maligned and misunderstood group, Frye resolutely classifies himself among the *Odyssey* critics. In the history of criticism there has prevailed a more or less tacit assumption that dictates that the "serious" critic should work primarily on texts partaking of what Matthew Arnold called "high seriousness." Much of contemporary criticism, in Frye's view, is still hampered by an implicit hierarchy of genres, with romance usually ending up at the bottom of the heap: "Any serious discussion of romance has to take into account its curiously proletarian status as a form generally disapproved of, in most ages, by the guardians of taste and learning, except when they use it for their own purposes. The close connection of the romantic and the popular runs through all literature."[1]

The simple fact that Frye is an *Odyssey* critic would be of limited interest, were it not that this predilection for comedy and romance turns out to have important consequences for literary theory. In moving from the *Anatomy of Criticism* to the *The Secular Scripture,* his most extended study of the structure of romance, one is not simply moving from theoretical to practical criticism. Not only are theoretical principles never very far from Frye's mind in any of his writings, romance is of strategic importance for the theory of literature in general, insofar as it forces reconsideration of many commonplace notions of mimesis and literary history.

Already in the *Anatomy,* the centrality of romance to Frye's scheme was clear, but the confines of systematic exposition left little room for a full-scale treatment of the mode. *The Secular Scripture,* based on lectures delivered at Harvard during his tenure as the Charles Eliot Norton Professor of Poetry, dilates considerably on the outline of romance presented in the *Anatomy*. And it is hardly a criticism of *The Secular Scripture* to say that it represents no theoretical advance over the work that preceded it by almost two decades. What is new in the later work is the expansiveness of its reference and the range of local insights that simply had no place in the skeletal exposition of the *Anatomy*.

The Secular Scripture retains in its published form the tone and texture of public lectures—which Frye elsewhere calls a "fantastically difficult genre"—and this lecture format produces a simpler, more popular style, one that coincides with the popularity of his subject matter. (Although Frye's presentation is simple in style, it is by no means simplistic in conceptual terms. Here and in many of his other books the "concessions" to the audience that grew out of lectures are largely those of technical vocabulary.) Frye begins with the modest, lapidary claim that his book "is concerned with some principles of storytelling" (*SS*, 3). The emphasis will be on romance fiction, in its naive and sentimental (or self-conscious) forms, though romance is by no means limited to fiction. As was proposed in the *Anatomy*, romance is a mode as well as a genre, and as a mode it will intersect with any number of genres, whether lyric, epic, or dramatic. Milton's "Il Penseroso" and "L'Allegro" lyrics, Shakespeare's *The Winter's Tale,* and Homer's *Odyssey* all lie equally within the compass of Frye's romance.

For many readers, the novel is the paradigm for fiction as well as for literature in general, and some of romance's "proletarian status" derives from it being considered as if it were an aberrant form of the novel. But Frye demonstrates convincingly how the romance is a much older, a more primitive form than that of the novel, with well-established conventions of its own. "The conventions of prose romance," Frye can claim with unparalleled authority, "show little change over the course of the centuries, and conservatism of this kind is the mark of a stable genre" (*SS*, 4).

The opposition between novel and romance seems at first a stable one, but the more one investigates the characteristics of romance, the more one realizes that romance inhabits, as it were, the novel form in the first place. Coming to the novel with a full awareness of the mechanisms of romance, one recognizes to what extent the novel is not so much opposed to romance as a *displaced* version of it. In the work of Sir Walter Scott, for example, one finds a realistic appeal to the representation of the world and historical events (which would make him a key figure for Lukacs and other Marxist aestheticians), but that appeal to the representation of history is made from within the structure of romance. In Scott we see again and again the same "building blocks" of romance: "light and dark heroines, outlawed or secret societies, wild women chanting prophecies, heroes of mysterious and ultimately fortunate birth" (SS, 5). Romance, as was indicated in the *Anatomy*, pays little attention to the canons of plausibility: the stories it tells are governed by desire rather than logic or reference to the real. The genre demands of the reader, at least provisionally, what Coleridge called a willing suspension of disbelief. In his anatomizing survey of romance through the course of many centuries, Frye chooses to focus on structural similarities: it should be noted, however, that the very structural stability of the genre could be the starting point for a more historicist or Marxist reading attentive to the historical specificity of particular romances, a challenge that has been taken up by several critics in the wake of Frye's work.[2]

In the first essay of the *Anatomy,* romance had figured as the primary mode of displaced myth (in the semi-historical sequence: myth, romance, high mimetic, low mimetic, irony). In *The Secular Scripture,* romance is once again considered in relation to myth both in the sense of a story of the gods and, more simply, as plot or narrative. Romance, even in its most "sentimental" forms, has its roots in myth in the former sense of a story of a divine being, as well as in popular folktales and fables, broadly understood. Myths and fables are similar in structure, the principal difference being that myths tend to stick together to form a mythology. In one sense, the project of *The Secular Scripture* is to unsettle the distinction between myth and secular fables:

We saw that there is no structural principle to prevent the fables of secular literature from also forming a mythology, or even a mythological universe. Is it possible, then, to look at secular stories as a whole, and as forming a single, integrated vision of the world, parallel to the Christian and biblical vision? This is the question implied in the "secular scripture" of my title. In the chapters that follow I should like to look at fiction as a total verbal order, with the outlines of an imaginative universe also in it. The Bible is the epic of the creator, with God as its hero. Romance is the structural core of all fiction: being directly descended from folktale, it brings us closer than any other aspect of literature to the sense of fiction, considered as a whole, as the epic of the creature, man's vision of his own life as a quest.

                                                                    (SS, 15)

Romance, then, is not one genre among others but the paradigm, in however modulated or displaced a form, of all fiction.[3] And it is in part the putative universality of romance that constitutes its claim to being a "secular scripture." The phrase in Frye's title cuts both ways, and it may be that he disturbs almost everyone by it. For "believers" in the Bible or any other text-based religion, as well as for "believers" in the autonomy of literature, the idea of a secular scripture remains an oxymoron. It is Frye's attention to matters of rhetoric and structure that permits so provocative a juxtaposition, to the dismay of those who look to religious and literary texts, first and foremost, for their content.[4] But perhaps the more questionable aspect of Frye's question about the relative status of scripture and romance is not whether secular romance parallels the Christian and biblical vision but whether those secular stories indeed form "a single integrated vision of the world"?

One possible way to distinguish between sacred and secular texts is in terms of their truth. The history of philosophy and literature features numerous examples of attempts to distinguish neatly between the truth of the sacred and the fiction of the secular, as when Plato tries to sever myth from fable or the New Testament *logos* from *mythos*. But however crucial these differences are in some contexts, they remain peripheral for the literary critic interested in rhetoric and structure. The structural similarities between myth and fable, sacred and secular scriptures, cannot be explained away by dogmatic fiat. In Frye's view, "truth" and "falsity" simply are not of much use as categories appropriate to the analytical understanding of literature. One other, less slippery, criterion exists that may help distinguish the mythical from the fabulous, namely differences in authority and social function. Such differences in function are easily legible in the annals of history, literary and otherwise. But, from the viewpoint of Frye's literary criticism, these differences are precisely those that are arbitrarily imposed and it is one task of rhetorical analysis to unsettle the apparently sharp distinctions between them.

When Frye turns, at the opening of his second chapter, to the theoretical framework of his study, he returns, as so often in the *Anatomy*, to the *Poetics* of Aristotle. To Aristotelian criticism, in Frye's view, we owe the axiom that art imitates nature as well as the distinction between form and content. Taken together, they suggest that "art is the form, and the nature which the art imitates is its content, so in literature art imitates nature by containing it internally" (*SS*, 35). There is nothing natural about art, then, except for its content, and content is not at all the essence of art. To say that art is the "container" of nature is not to relapse in a version of the mimetic fallacy that holds that art is a reflection of reality.[5] The history or romance, more than any other mode, shows that it has little or nothing to do with the direct representation of reality:

The change of taste in favor of romance raises a good many questions about the validity of some common critical assumptions about fiction which have been fostered by the prestige of a displaced and realistic tradition. There is still a strong tendency to avoid problems of technique and design and structure in fiction, and to concentrate on what the book talks about rather than on what it actually presents. It is still not generally understood either that "reality" in literature cannot be presented at all except within the conventions of literary structure, and that those conventions must be understood first.

(SS, 43)

Romance is riddled with the "unnatural" and the "unreal," and thus would seem to rank among the purest products of the imagination. But what does this freest of faculties produce? According to Frye, it tends when left by itself "to produce the rigidly conventionalized" (SS, 36). The word *conventional* here should not be understood in a political or ethical sense: at the level of structure, a guerrilla theater production is as conventionalized as any Harlequin romance.[6]

The form of romance so dominates its changing content that it always emerges as formulaic, incessantly returning to the same motifs, themes, and even metaphors. Romance, like all mimetic literature, is an imitation of action, even if the action imitated could never take place in real life. Romance tends to represent ritual acts that are "symbolic and representative of human life in a more universal perspective" (SS, 55), ritual events such as weddings and funerals whose main function is to provide society with a sense of coherence. Frye is often taken to task by leftist criticism for his focus on timeless structures and universal perspectives, but he is well aware that similar rhetorical and narrative strategies can be enlisted in a variety of historically specific ways:

In a medieval chivalric romance the jousts and tournaments, the centripetal movement of knights to Arthur's or Charlemagne's court and their dispersal out from it into separate quests, the rescued damsels and beloved ladies, the giants and helpful or perilous beasts, all form a ritualized action expressing the ascendancy of a horse-riding aristocracy. They also express the aristocracy's dreams of its own social function, and the idealized acts of protection and responsibility that it invokes to justify its function. The same thing is true of all ages of romance, from the Cinderella and industrious-apprentice romances of bourgeois aggressiveness to the adventure stories of Rider Haggard and John Buchan and Rudyard Kipling which incorporate the dreams of British imperialism. This is the process of what we called "kidnapping" romance, the absorbing of it into the ideology of an ascendant class.

(*SS,* 56–57)

Romance may not "refer to" or "represent" real states of affairs in the world, but that does not mean it is not caught up in a network of changing historical relations of power and domination. Nonetheless, Frye's concern, as much strategic as philosophical, is first and foremost with issues of literary structure: "it is precisely the elementary facts of structure that we are inclined to overlook, and the social facts that we tend to exaggerate" (*SS,* 78). And nowhere more than in romance are the elements of literary structure so open to analysis. Frye invokes the insight of Oscar Wilde's *The Decay of Lying* to argue that romance, more than all other genres, points to what is literary about literature: the way it gives shape to life which, as such, has none.[7] This recognition becomes strategic for the theory of literature, because romance stands as both the displacement of myth and the material for its own displacement in what is called realism: hence romance becomes, in Frye's schema, "central" for the history and theory of literature as a whole.

One way realistic narrative displaces its romantic counterpart is to render its sequences "logical" and "rational": the word "hence" may be thought of as the exemplary connective of realist fiction, as opposed to the simple "and then" of romance. But the logic of realist fiction is just that, a fiction. The literary critic, in Frye's view, "deals only with rhetoric, and one of the functions of rhetoric is to present an *illusion* of logic and causality" (*SS,* 48). Nonetheless, some of the differences between realism and romance are as real as literary differences can be: "The realist, with his sense of logical and horizontal continuity, leads us up to the end of his story; the romancer, scrambling over a series of disconnected episodes, seems to be trying to get us to the top of it" (*SS,* 50). Though Frye's metaphor seems to come out of the blue, so to speak, the emphasis on verticality will lead to important insights into characterization in romance.

In the mode of romance, as opposed to the novel, one finds less a sense of character "development" (a particularly bourgeois myth that survives most notably in popular film criticism) than a polarization between characters. Here the ambiguities of moral life have been simplified to the point where characters are either good *or* bad. Hence we have the sense of verticality in romance, whose characters occupy slots in paradigm columns of good and evil. Frye draws on the Dantesque distinction between force and fraud (*forza* and *froda*) to underscore the way the romance tradition relies so heavily on the latter. The distinction in fact goes back, as he notes, to the two epics of Homer, exemplified in the difference between the wrath of Achilles in the *Iliad* and the guile of Ulysses in the *Odyssey*. This distinction in genre—between realism and tragedy on the one hand and comedy and romance on the other—turns in part on a distinction in gender. Since female characters typically have less sheer force at their disposal than their male counterparts, they are forced to rely on fraud, guile, craft, and cunning. None of these are peculiarly female characteristics but do point to a special alliance between romance and certain literary and historical determinations of the feminine. Frye, following Samuel Butler and others, permits himself some speculation about the possibility of a Penelope-centered version of the *Odyssey* that would have preceded the version that has come down to us. In tragedy from Euripides onward, women tend to be victims rather than forceful agents, whereas in romance they generally take on a much more active role. Even in the Ulysses-centered *Odyssey,* Penelope plays a central part in the furthering—and the delay—of the epic's main action.

Romance is the genre that most clearly presents the projection of desires, and chief among them is the erotic. The romance, for Frye, is "almost by definition" a love story. The trajectory of romance is toward erotic consummation, but however devoutly that consummation is to be wished, it must always be deferred, at least temporarily. Romance takes time, primarily the time of what Milton calls "sweet, reluctant, amorous delay." This means that much of the action in romance is taken up with the temporary frustration of desire: hence the seemingly inordinate importance of the themes of virginity and chastity, from the plight of Penelope in the *Odyssey* to that Pamela in Richardson's novel of that name. (Here we see the force of Frye's structural analysis, namely, the way he can show how often the content of a text is motivated by formal considerations, and not simply by "experience.") Though the heroine figures prominently in romance, the genre is by no means a monument to women's liberation. Romance heroines are often sacrificial victims and if they happen to survive they are sometimes married off to the very men to whom they were "sacrificed" in the first place. Romance is in Frye's view very much the product of a "male-dominated world," with all its attendant double standards and strategies of oppression.

The emphasis in romance on heroism, suffering, and the delay of erotic fulfillment suggests parallels with the Christian myth, the story of a superhuman act of sacrifice that leads ultimately to the hero's wedding to his bride, that is, Christ's marriage to the church as foretold in Revelation. But secular romance, of course, is not bound by the same doctrinal constraints as scripture. Moreover, Frye contends that romance cannot be thought to "derive" from the Christian myth, hence its unorthodox status as a purely secular scripture.

From the discussion of character Frye circles back to the question of plot, though as modern critics as distinct as Henry James and Vladimir Propp have recognized, character is to a considerable extent a function of plot. There are, in Frye's view, only so many ways a romantic hero or heroine can go. In fact, there are only four narrative movements possible in all of literature: "first, the descent from a higher world; second, the descent to a lower world; third, the ascent from a lower world; and fourth, the ascent to a higher world. All stories in literature are complications of, or metaphorical derivations from, these four narrative radicals" (*SS*, 97). Ascent and descent are foregrounded in romance more than most other genres because romance typically begins its action with "some kind of break in consciousness," whether sleeping, dreaming, or forgetting. This break in consciousness usually signals a departure from the world of ordinary experience, up into an idealized realm, an Elysium or Eden, or down into a hellish nightmare. In myth proper, the descent is typically that of a god to the world of experience, the way Jesus descends from the heavens to take on human form. The most radical movements of myth are displaced in romance, so that the action remains within the margins of probability, with only some of nature's laws suspended. Thus, instead of a descent from the heavens or to the underworld, one may find a fall in social status, often the starting point for romantic and comic action. The whole range of descents, in their variously displaced forms, are charted in a chapter entitled "The Bottomless Dream: Themes of Descent."[8] It soon becomes clear that descent is not necessarily a negative movement: each of the four levels of the mythological universe can be positively or negatively marked. But the descent is, most typically, to a labyrinthine world of horror, cruelty, or alienation. With respect to character, the descent is often the movement that accompanies a loss of identity, a loss which in most romance plots constitutes only a temporary detour on the road to a recovery of that "same" identity. As well as a hellish labyrinth, the underworld can be the site of secret knowledge, especially knowledge of the future, as it is in the descent of book 6 of Virgil's *Aeneid*. (The latter point offers still another example of how a given theme is motivated in terms of the plot, where concern for the future of the story is paramount.) Equally important in the descent quest is knowledge of the past: countless romantic characters are in the dark about their own ancestry. Frye observes that Scott and Dickens (writers who are in part associated with the triumph of realism in the nineteenth century) "would often be helpless for plot interest without the motif of the mysterious birth" (*SS,* 101). The analysis of themes of ascent reveals very similar structures, patterns almost fearfully symmetrical. Thus, corresponding to the dark oracular voice of the underworld god, one finds a riddle, but a riddle with a solution.[9] Whereas the descent usually signals a confusion of identity and frustration of desire, the ascent is usually marked by a recovery of identity. The erotic quest typically culminates in an ascension to a higher level of reality, if not literally to another world above.

One could continue to catalog the parallels between descent and ascent narratives charted in *The Secular Scripture,* but it would be more revealing of what is at stake in Frye's reading of romance to dwell on one example from the close of his lecture on the themes of ascent. There Frye appears simply to be completing his catalog with the analysis of yet another example in a series designed to convey the whole range of possibilities culled from the astonishing breadth of his reading. But the story Frye retells ascends, as it were, out of the narrative progression and attains a certain parabolic significance for his theory of criticism. The story is from the "Hymn of the Soul" in the apocryphal Acts of Thomas, and it merits quotation at some length:

The Soul says that when he was a child in the palace of his father, his parents provided him with money and jewels and sent him down to Egypt, where he was to find a pearl in the sea guarded by a serpent, and come back to his original state again. He also has a brother who remained in the upper world. The Soul disguises himself and descends, but his disguise is penetrated and he is persuaded to eat the food of the lower world, like Proserpine before him. This causes him to forget both his origin and his mission, and fall into a deep sleep. His Parents send a "letter" to him, the lowerworld oracle that we have met before; the Soul reads it, and as he reads his memory comes back. He puts the serpent to sleep, seizes the pearl, and starts back again. At the beginning of his quest he had been clothed in a garment which is clearly the form of his original identity. He meets this garment again and again and realizes that it is, in fact, his real self. He sees it "as it had been in a mirror," and it is brought him by twins, "Two, yet one shape was upon both." Putting it on, he makes his way back to his own world. Like Apuleius' story, this is a story of the "Soul"; in other words it is the story of ourselves. Crucial to it is the role of the letter or message, which not only awakens him but is what draws him upward to his self-recognition. It seems that one becomes the ultimate hero of the great quest of man, not so much by virtue of what one does, as by virtue of what and how one reads.

(*SS*, 156–57)

It may be wishful thinking for Frye to identify the Soul so categorically with "ourselves" but he is certainly right to recognize himself in this scene of romance reading. All along Frye had demonstrated that romance was much concerned with metamorphosis and the confusion of identity. And then suddenly Frye rewrites the romance scenario by substituting the reader for the hero, or, more precisely, by inscribing the reader as the hero. The garment, a traditional figure for the figural, is here equally a metaphor for the text, for it is in the reading of the literary text that our very identity is at stake. One implication of this allegory of reading is that the critical quest is itself a romance, and that Frye's particular quest is then, as the self-reflexive passage just cited suggests, a romance of romance.[10]

But if the reader is implicated in the allegory of romance, this relation is not merely one of identification with the idealized characters of hero and heroine. Indeed, for Frye, "this identifying process is something to be outgrown" (*SS*, 162). Reading is ultimately less an act of identification than of translation and one of the centrifugal movements of reading is outward to the world of politics and social action. Does romance as a genre have an identifiable politics? Or can this single genre be mobilized in political programs of utterly different kinds? Frye had observed earlier that the tone and setting of romance was often that of aristocratic snobbery at the same time that it had an undeniably "proletarian" function at the bottom of the heap of literary genres. What is it about romance that permits both Walter Scott the Tory and William Morris the socialist to excel at it in equal degrees? Scott's success in this respect may be deceiving, at least in terms of ideological persuasion. In Frye's view, the most compelling aspects of Scott's narratives are precisely those that depart from the official Tory position that is supposed to override everything else in his work. Frye believes there is a more genuine "link between the revolutionary and the romantic" (SS, 165). This does not mean that all romance literature will be progressive in political terms; indeed, Frye can speak of "a conservative, mystical strain of social and religious acceptance" that "runs all through romance" (SS, 171). But the movement of romance is, however fanciful, ultimately in the direction of a liberation from oppression or repression, regardless of whether that movement goes against the grain of an author's express political program.[11] Curiously, it is in commenting on the politics of romance that Frye's own thought verges on the indecisive. Indeed, the following is one of the few sentences in Frye's work that appears muddled: "It is possible that social, and political, or religious revolution always, and necessarily, betrays a revolutionary ideal of which the imagination holds the secret" (SS, 165). The words "possible" and "necessarily" coexist uneasily in this sentence, as if two of Frye's voices were struggling for possession of a single thought. Frye has shown how much of literature has the character of a hypothetical postulate and clearly criticism too partakes of this discursive mode. The necessity of the betrayal of revolutionary ideals is stated in a declarative mode, but that necessity is only introduced as a possibility. It would be a mistake to read this passage simply as a betrayal of Frye's own revolutionary ideals, for such a recognition, even when stated in equivocal fashion, is still compatible with the Blakean and Miltonic ethos that informs so much of his work.

The romance might be seen as the human, fallen counterpart of the divine comedy, insofar as it projects its desires with a strong sense of the possibility of their not being fulfilled. But it is of course the drive to fulfillment that characterizes the romance plot, whether or not those desires are satisfied. Some characteristics of romance then are transhistorical, which does not mean that romance is cut off from history or our sense of it. Frye observes that "the frequent association of romance with the historical, such as we see in the Waverly novels, is based, I should think, on the principle that there is a peculiar emotional intensity in contemplating something, including our own earlier lives, that we know we have survived" (SS, 176). Moreover, it is not that romance simply runs counter to the force of history: as Henry James suggests in his study of Hawthorne, romance "supplements" history rather than contradicts it.[12] The suspension of natural law in romance is itself always inscribed as a historical gesture in the moment of the text's production, one of the two historical moments to which a critic must attend, the other being the moment of reading.

Much of the power of the Bible, the grand divine comedy, derives from the inclusion of its readers in the story, whether or not they believe in it. The story that stretches from the beginning to the end of time encompasses every individual story, however abstractly. The appeal of romance is similar insofar as it too turns out to be about its readers: as Frye says, "the message of all romance is *de te fabula:* the story is about you; and it is the reader who is responsible for the way literature functions, both socially and individually" (*SS,* 186). This last phrase suggests that the critic, even more than the casual reader, is implicated in the romance scenario, the quest for individual and social fulfillment, whose movement is ideally comic and revolutionary. This movement of romance carries over into the final chapter of *The Secular Scripture,* entitled "The Recovery of Myth," a phrase with a double resonance. Recovery of identity is the archetypal pattern of romance and thus it is myth in the fundamental sense of narrative or plot. But "the recovery of myth" equally describes Frye's own critical quest, with his goal being the reinstatement of myth as the central category of literary criticism.

The Secular Scripture remains Frye's fullest statement on the romance, but some aspects of his treatment of the genre and mode are obscured by the presentation in the confines of that book. In particular, one misses the sense of how the study of genre can illuminate a specific historical conjunction. Frye's *A Study of English Romanticism,* published well before *The Secular Scripture,* is a work that could be said to put the romance back into romanticism. We recall from *Fearful Symmetry* and the *Anatomy of Criticism* the pervasiveness of a stubborn structure that organizes what Frye calls the mythological universe. This universe, in Frye's reconstruction, consists of four levels: at the top, the realm of God or the gods from which authority descends; next, a paradisal but sublunary world of innocence; next, the mortal world of ordinary experience; and last and least, hell or the underworld. The structure of this universe remains fairly constant for literature of the West from the period of classical antiquity and the Hebrew Bible up to the end of the eighteenth century. But then one begins to witness an important change in literary sensibility that is paralleled by a structural change in the mythological universe. A principal sign of the times is the change in the movement of authority. In the older scheme of things, authority descended from above, exemplified in God's descent from the

clouds. In the new dispensation, authority, power, and energy are located "downward," within the self. Many of the images formerly associated with the underworld are now overturned and positively
marked: Prometheus rather than Zeus is the presiding deity of romanticism, and a poet like William Blake can refer to many of his poetic
projects as fragments of a "Bible in Hell." Thus the structure of the
new mythological universe is inflected very differently with respect to
the characters who inhabit it. The most salient change concerns the
source of authority, for it is now widely recognized that what was
thought to be the power of the gods turns out to be the product of the
mind's projection, especially the mind of the poet. The movement of
the romantic quest is now as much downward and inward as it was
formerly upward and outward. [13]

In the domain of literary history, as well as that of literary theory,
Frye's predilection for romance produces important revisionary results.
Frye claims in *A Study of English Romanticism* to conduct a series of
exemplary readings, preceded by a general essay on "The Romantic
Myth." But his choices of the exemplary go against the grain of the
romantic canon that was being codified by his contemporaries. The
three works singled out for sustained attention are Shelley's *Prometheus
Unbound,* Keats's *Endymion,* and Beddoes's *Death's Jest-Book.* Of the
three, only *Prometheus Unbound* was likely to turn up on an academic
syllabus in romantic literature. Beddoes remains virtually unread by
popular audiences and untouched by scholars. And *Endymion* is considered something of a failed, ambitious project that simply cannot com-
pete with the perfection of Keats's odes. Yet Frye succeeds in showing
that these works reveal something important about the rewriting of the
mythological universe during the romantic period. Frye's critical concerns have never been primarily evaluative, and the focus on myth and
structure permits a reading of romanticism that goes well beyond the
competing versions of the period offered in his day, most of which were
anchored in Wordsworth's *Prelude* as the epic of the sublime self.

No discussion of Frye's reading of romance would be complete without attention to the extraordinary status accorded in his work to Shakespeare's exemplary experiments in the mode of romance. The romances,
as a whole, are among the least "popular" and least performed plays of
Shakespeare, with the possible exception of *The Tempest.* [14] But again
Frye's primary interest is in literary structure. He is, in general, supremely uninterested in matters of biographical criticism—Shakespeare, of course, has been the victim of an absurd amount of such

criticism. Paradoxically, the very absence of any full account of Shakespeare the man has fueled the imaginations of scores of second-rate critics.[15] One of the few important things one can establish with relative certainty about Shakespeare's life is the sequence of the plays he wrote. Precise knowledge about the sequence is of course impossible, but one can demonstrate a tendency toward romance in the movement from early to late Shakespeare; indeed, Frye can speak of Shakespeare's "logical evolution toward romance."[16] Though Shakespeare is for Frye a supremely "disinterested" writer, the tendency toward romance shows an increasing interest in the structure of drama per se.[17] The writing of romance for Shakespeare involves experimentation with the very limits of the dramatic genre: the romances are at once self-reflexive, theater about theater, and extraordinarily comprehensive in that they contain both tragic and comic action in a single movement. The romances present a "drama beyond drama, a kind of ultimate confrontation of the human community with an artistic realization of itself."[18] Thus the recognition staged within romance functions as an analogue or allegory of our experience of romance with its unnerving entanglement of art and life. The late plays of Shakespeare, like all romances, hold up a broken mirror, a mirror in which the reader glimpses not nature but him- or her-self caught in a romantic act.

Chapter Four
The Function of Criticism at Any Given Time: Literature, Education, and Society

To judge by much of the reception of the *Anatomy of Criticism,* Frye seems a critic fixed almost exclusively on the structure and texture of literature, with little concern for the larger social forces in and by which the literary text is inscribed. The *Anatomy*'s doctrine that poems come from other poems appears to short-circuit any attempt to connect text and event, literature and society. I attempted to show in chapter 2 to what extent this view of Frye did not do justice to the text of the *Anatomy* as a whole. And when one turns to work written before and especially after the *Anatomy,* one finds a pervasive concern with precisely the issues Frye is thought to have avoided. Part of the confusion, no doubt, can be ascribed to Frye's mode of presentation, and perhaps in particular to his penchant for paradox. When one looks somewhat closer at the context of the dictum that poems come from poems, one finds not an ivory-tower aestheticism that contemplates literature in a self-contained universe, but an analysis of the conventionality of literary forms which is unthinkable outside a larger set of social conventions.[1] Moreover, the final essay of the *Anatomy* reiterates a pattern, one which organizes the critical philosophy of Kant among others, whereby the literary or aesthetic is a bridge from the sphere of knowledge to that of ethics. And just as the literary tends ultimately toward the ethical, so criticism aims in the end toward a certain praxis, to say nothing of its being "practical" in the first place. As Frye says in a programmatic essay on "The Responsibilities of the Critic": "The critic is there, not so much to explain the poet, as to translate literature into a continuous dialogue with society."[2]

Frye's earliest published writings were reviews written mostly for the *Canadian Forum,* a journal of political and cultural criticism with a low budget and a high caliber of writing. During the first fifteen or so years of Frye's association with the *Canadian Forum,* the journal was aligned with the Co-Operative Commonwealth Federation (CCF), a democratic-socialist party with its roots in the United Church of Canada and, further back, in the tradition of Protestant dissent in Britain.[3] An earlier incarnation of *Canadian Forum* had been called the *Rebel* and the later version retained much of its oppositional and iconoclastic program. The *Forum* was a leading intellectual organ of the Canadian Left, especially of the trade-union movement, and its pages featured some of the best poetry and criticism being written in the decades between the depression and the cold war. Frye began contributing reviews to the *Forum* in 1936, and as of 1946 he joined the editorial board, becoming managing editor—the highest position on the staff—in 1948. He served as managing editor until 1952, during which time the *Forum* attained a greater degree of autonomy from the CCF, becoming, in Frye's words, an independent journal.[4] Frye's writings for the *Forum* were mainly literary, though he also contributed numerous editorials of a directly political nature, such as several suspicious of cold war, anticommunist hysteria in the United States. He could begin one editorial with a reference to "the quaint old writer" Karl Marx on the subject of technology and social change, meaning that Marx is not necessarily old or quaint.

As a reviewer, Frye faced in a particularly pressing way the question of the function of literature and the arts in society.[5] The academic study of literature can proceed in relative isolation from the reading public, but the reviewer must answer to a constituency larger and more varied than a group of peers who share certain specialized interests.[6] The questions "why write (this)?" and "why read (this)?" are raised implicitly or explicitly at every turn. Literary criticism, for Frye, has a special relation to education and the intellectual life of society that extends well beyond the boundaries of academia. It is special not by virtue of the fact the Frye happens to be a literary critic, but rather because at the center of literary criticism one finds the issues that radiate in every direction of the verbal universe. And without this verbal universe there would be no society to begin with.[7]

Frye's most extended meditation on the function of criticism in society is called *The Critical Path,* which began as a relatively modest essay for a conference. The talk soon evolved into a long essay published in a volume of *Daedalus* on education and the humanities, only to be expanded still more to form a book-length essay. *The Critical Path* begins with a question of itinerary, the titular phrase being an

echo of Kant's formulation for the "way" *(Weg)* of his critical philosophy. Behind Kant's phrasing lies a long tradition of metaphors for the
"way" of philosophy from Parmenides to Descartes and beyond. Indeed
the metaphor of the path or way is central to philosophical discourse,
beginning with the Greek term *odos,* which can never quite be disentangled from the philosophical notion of *methodos.*[8] But in Frye, as in
Descartes, the way of philosophy sometimes resembles the errant path
of the romantic hero. We saw in the previous chapter how Frye's critical
project was itself inscribed in something of a romantic plot, and the
same may be true of the critic's quest in *The Critical Path.* No sooner
does Frye invoke the idea of Kantian criticism, that seeks to steer a
middle course between dogmatism and skepticism, than he alludes,
without naming the source, to a "romantic" scenario straight out of
Dante: "About twenty-five years ago, when still in middle life, I lost
my way in the dark wood of Blake's prophecies, and looked around for
some path that would get me out of there."[9] The dark wood of Blakean
prophecy would in the end issue into the light of what Geoffrey Hartman calls, quoting Blake, Frye's "sweet science," the theoretical foundation most fully elaborated in the *Anatomy.*[10] The scientific project of
literary criticism cannot, at least in Frye's case, be disentangled from
the paradigmatic form of literature, the romance.

   The Critical Path takes up where the *Anatomy* left off, with questions
of rhetoric and the relation between writer and public, though Frye
reworks several steps of the *Anatomy's* argument in the more expansive,
meditative mode of public essay. In the *Anatomy,* Frye had complained
about the tendency of a certain kind of allegorical criticism to read
beyond rather than in poems, aligning the text with some extratextual
referent such as the poet's life or the historical events of his day. The
issue surfaces again in *The Critical Path* because when one begins to
think of the relations between literature and society, the categories of
reference and relevance soon appear. In Frye's view, the historical or
biographical critic's interest is ultimately in the content of art, whether
manifest or latent, and this same critic tends to read the literary text
primarily as a socially determined product. Several aspects of these
determinist programs are, for Frye, compelling. He sees that Marxism,
among other discourses, understands literature as part of the social
process that "forms the genuine context of literature" and notes further
that "Marxism takes a social view of literature which is comprehensive
enough to see it within this genuine context" (*CP,* 19). But there is

often a gap between Marxist theory and Marxist practice, which tends to read literature reductively through an allegorical interpretation of its social content.[11] Without due consideration of the formal qualities of literature, no literary criticism or literary history will be worth much more than the paper it is printed on. Convention is, in Frye's view, "a force even stronger than history": only a criticism conscious of the determinations of form and content within a larger social context could produce a "genuine history of literature" (*CP*, 23).[12]

If Frye in *The Critical Path* is something of a Dante, then Vico is surely his Virgil. Frye considers Giambattista Vico, an isolated and eccentric Italian intellectual of the early eighteenth century and author of *The New Science* (1744), to be "one of the very few thinkers to understand anything of the historical role of the poetic impulse in civilization as a whole" (*CP*, 34).[13] Vico saw that society could not get very far without a mythological framework and one or more canonical stories. His work was innovative particularly for its insight into stories of the gods as distinctly human cultural products. The more one studied mythology, the sooner one realized that the myths of the gods were less revelations about the divine than expressions of what Frye calls "the myth of concern." That is to say that the myths told more about their authors than about their ostensible topics. In speaking of a myth of concern in the singular, Frye follows a tendency in Vico to see humans as being of one mind, speaking essentially one language, despite differences of history and nationality.[14] And it is this penchant in Frye to sum up a whole range of historically variegated data in a single pattern that most unsettles his historicist critics. Though there is, strictly speaking, no single myth of concern that could be articulated, what Frye, in Kantian fashion, points to in the use of such categories is the condition of possibility of any historically specific myths. This means that one does not have to choose between "myth" and "history": they are not mutually exclusive categories. But it is one thing to acknowledge this in theory and another to maintain a practice of criticism consonant with it. At times, Frye's cultural criticism displays a certain rush toward mythologizing that does indeed obscure the historical event or text that archetypal criticism is supposed to illuminate.[15] Though Frye at one moment can speak of a single "myth of concern," it soon becomes evident that not everyone shares this myth equally: "In every structured society the ascendant class attempts to take over the myth of concern and make it, or an essential part of it, a rationalization of its ascendancy" (*CP,* 49). Thus Frye acknowledges, like Vico before him, something like class struggle at the level of myth.

Of the contending political myths in Western civilization, Frye is most intrigued and attracted by "the revolutionary myth," for which the paradigm is the Christian Bible. The Christian myth never quite merges with that of the ascendant class, a fact that marks one of its affinities with another great revolutionary myth of the West elaborated in Marxism. Indeed, Frye's mythological abstraction enables him to locate three characteristics common to Christianity and Marxism: 1) a unique historical revelation; 2) a canon of essential and approved texts; and 3) a resistance to "revisionism" (*CP,* 51). The counterpoint of Christianity and Marxism comes almost to inform Frye's style, as for example when he is discussing the line of succession in the Gospels. There he can speak of "such figures as Paul, whose letters, like the pamphlets of Lenin later, deal with specific tactical decisions in a way that leads to far-reaching theoretical principles" (*CP,* 121). What can Christians and Marxists make of such a proposition? Like his title, *The Secular Scripture,* Frye's formulation here risks alienating the two constituencies it brings together in a single sentence. His rhetoric forces consideration of one's own mythology from a disinterested perspective (as far as that is possible), which is precisely what goes against the grain of most ideologies.[16]

One reason that there are contending political myths in the first place is that society invariably manifests a certain "tension between concern and freedom" (*CP,* 55). In searching for the delicate balance of concern and freedom that would be most beneficial for society, Frye turns not to classical political theory but to the subgenre of the defence of poetry, specifically to the examples of Sidney and Shelley, the former a Renaissance and the latter a romantic theorist.[17] The tremendous advance of writing culture (in what came to be called by a colleague of Frye's "the Gutenberg Galaxy") posed a threat to the survival of poetry. Hence the need to write so many defences of it. For Sidney and many of his contemporaries, the Renaissance poet had been cut off from an ancient and authentic tradition in which the poet was among the founders of civilization, the equal of the statesman and philosopher. One possible reason for this separation emerges as early as in the writings of Plato, where it is argued that poets have a more attenuated relation to truth than do philosophers. What then is the use of poetry? Frye reconstructs Sidney's humanist program in this way: "The function of poetry . . . is to provide a *rhetorical analogue* to concerned truth. Rhetoric, said Aristotle, is the *antistrophos,* the answering chorus, of truth, and whatever genuine social function the poet has depends on the consonance between his rhetoric and the rational disciplines, with their more exact relation to reality" (*CP,* 66). The poet, in Sidney's conception, gives us a "second nature," or alternatively, a golden world, the ideal or romanticized one in which we would want to live. If poetry is to be defended for its truth, it cannot (and need not) be based on the narrow conception of truth as the correspondence between words and things.

Though Milton wrote no formal defence of poetry, his whole life and works were an implicit defence of it. For Milton the sources of authority were to be sought in the inspired words of God, and the role of the poet was the re-creation of that divine word for society. Much of the spirit of Milton's position is carried over into Shelley's *Defence of Poetry.* Shelley was, of course, in a quite different ideological position from Milton: he was, in some sense, an atheist (though one, as Mary Shelley recounts, who read the Bible every day), and his vision of the poet is as a secular prophet and more. Man is the creator of his own society and the poet's voice is the only oracle still functioning. Shelley, like Sidney before him, seeks to restore the lost heritage of the poet as the lawgiver for society. In Frye's survey of the changing function of poet, one thing remains virtually constant: namely, that poetry never quite loses touch with its original foundation in a sense of social concern. But this concern cannot simply be translated into a corpus of beliefs or dogma. Frye follows Sidney in maintaining that, in a paradoxical way, the poet affirms nothing. What is crucial in poetry is not the explicit beliefs it may profess but its presentation of theses and hypotheses, postulates for *the way the world could be* rather than descriptions of *the way it is.*

One of the theoretical insights of criticism (which is equally one of the conditions of its possibility) is that beliefs can be held and subjected to scrutiny at the same time. And indeed, in Frye's view, it is the responsibility of all imaginative and reflective people, not just critics, to do so. Literature, then, plays a special role in education because it incorporates as well as provokes a certain suspension of belief. As Frye says: "Literature is the embodiment of a language, not of belief or of thought: it will say anything, and therefore in a sense it says nothing. It provides the technical resources for formulating the myths of concern, but does not itself formulate: for formulation we must turn from literature back to the myths of concern themselves" (*CP*, 101).

The most conspicuous example of a myth of concern in the Western tradition is the Judaeo-Christian Bible. In the wake of the Enlightenment, the Bible became the object of a "crisis in belief" arising from the submission of the biblical text to the canons of evidence and rationality required in the discipline of history. But literary criticism helps demonstrate how inadequate are questions about "belief" in the representational or referential accuracy of the Bible. Frye can even conclude that the Bible is "much closer to being a work of literature than it is to being a work of history or doctrine" (*CP*, 116). The question of belief, then, is shifted from a merely epistemological affair, concerned with what we think or know to be the case, to the pragmatic concerns of ethics, morals, and politics. Frye contends that "what we really believe is not what we say or think we believe but what our actions show we believe, and no belief which is not an axiom of behavior is a genuinely concerned belief" (*CP*, 112).

Myths of concern are not simply "literary," insofar as they inform a whole range of existential, historical, and political texts, but as myths they always contain one element which is irreducibly literary. Frye remarks that from "a literary point of view every statement of belief or concern can be seen as the moral of a fable" (*CP*, 123). In the *Anatomy* Frye had argued that one cannot "teach literature," but only literary criticism; even so, the teacher of literature is to some extent the medium of the text. Frye recalls in *The Critical Path* the example from *Paradise Lost* of the angels' instruction of Adam through fable, and intimates that Milton's angels should set the example for mere mortal teachers. Teaching via the fable has certain consequences for the function of literature in society, for it entails the "responsibilities of a greater freedom, including the responsibility of rejecting censorship" (*CP*, 125).[18] Frye puts the *liber* (or book) back into "liberal" education, for the freedom of society depends on an environment in which books can circulate freely. In reading Frye's literary criticism, it is often difficult to tell precisely where his ideological sympathies lie, but here and elsewhere Frye clearly sides with the Milton of *Areopagitica*, the Milton for whom freedom in reading and writing was the sine qua non of a genuine society.

Literary criticism is, of course, not limited to democratic, egalitarian societies, but both the book and the institution of criticism have special relations to those social forms. Frye posits that the critical element in education "consists in becoming increasingly aware of one's own mythological conditioning" (*CP*, 135); we should recall that Frye suggests the word "ideological" may be substituted for "mythological." Ideally, and often in practice, such an awareness of one's own conditioning leads to a toleration of other positions. Thus criticism contributes to the grandest project of democracy, which consists in giving equal rights to all citizens (*CP*, 138). This is not, of course, to say that in societies that are technically democratic there are not antidemocratic forces at work. And any rigorous practice of censorship will reverse nearly all the benefits afforded by a literate culture. The book is by no means a political cure-all, but when functioning freely it is an instrument particularly appropriate to the process of democracy.

   The Critical Path was written in the wake of the student protests of the late 1960s and is clearly marked by the experience of that historical moment. Frye spent a term at the University of California at Berkeley in 1969 and had witnessed firsthand one of the most highly charged conflicts of its kind. Frye notes that many social protests of the period were in part a return to the mechanisms and rituals of oral culture. In this period even more than others, it was impossible (and undesirable) for the critic to ignore "the social context of his subject" (*CP*, 147). Frye's critical writings are replete with insights into the social context of literature, but here one instance of his application of archetypal criticism to a social event leaves something to be desired:

An example that I witnessed recently was the extraordinary sleepwalking ritual of the "people's park" crisis in Berkeley in the summer of 1969. Here a vacant lot with a fence around it became assimilated to the archetype of the expulsion of Eden, dramatizing the conflict of the democratic community and the oligarchical conspiracy in a pastoral mode related to some common conventions of the Western story. A student editorial informed us that the lot was "covered with blood" because, like all the rest of the land in North America, it had been stolen from the Indians (murder of Abel archetype). The expelling angels in this symbolism were (as in Blake's version of it) demonic, and the police, with their helmets and bayonets and gas masks, were endeavouring, with considerable success, to represent the demonic in its popular science fiction form, of robots or bug-eyed monsters from outer space.

(*CP*, 146)

Not all of this "archetypalizing" is Frye's own, but he takes up where the student editorial leaves off and provides his own reading of the spectacle. What begins as a parody of the student editorial turns into something of a parody of archetypal criticism, for Frye's ingenuity here appears beside the point of this political crisis. This incident was much on Frye's mind in the time following his Berkeley tenure: it came up again and again in his numerous convocation addresses. In one of these addresses, Frye applies a different and more persuasive sort of criticism to the event, noting, for example, that the police in Berkeley were guilty of "rioting" and that one could no longer think in terms of the riot being controlled by "law and order."[19] But whatever the infelicities of the example cited above, it is incidents like these that prompt Frye's declaration on the peril of ignoring the social context of literature.

The pressures of society may well force the literary critic to be conscious of the historical and political context of literature, but social thought is, as Frye suggested in the *Anatomy*, literary in the first place. The two great organizing myths of political discourse are the social contract and the Utopia, the forms that address the origin and end of history, its *arche* and *telos*. The origins and ends of society are not simply open for inspection in any empirically reliable way, which leads one to suspect that something else is at stake in the texts that conjure up the social contract and the Utopia. Frye proposes that the great political thinkers, such as Plato, More, Locke, and Rousseau, are in fact writing largely about the theory of education.[20] Their myths are to some extent expendable, whereas the promotion of argument and use of critical reason are not. Frye speaks less of the social than of the "educational contract" (*CP,* 163) that creates a source of spiritual authority in society.[21] The word "authority" has a sinister ring to some, as it did to many of the student protesters of the sixties and seventies. But authority need not be authoritarian. Frye's plea is for a critical path that winds its way between dogmatism and skepticism, in political as well as literary matters. In an alternative formulation that sums up much of the itinerary, Frye writes: "So we come back to where our critical path began, in the contrast between an existing world and a world which may not exist but is pointed to by the articulate orders of experience, the intelligible world of the thinker and the imaginative world of the artist, which are or seem to be analogies of it" (*CP,* 168).

Soon after William Hazlitt met the young but already legendary Coleridge he was taken with the curious path this great poet and critic followed: "I observed that he continually crossed me on the way by shifting from one side of the footpath to the other. This struck me as an odd movement; but I did not at that time connect it with any instability of purpose or involuntary change of principle, as I have done since."[22] In *The Critical Path,* Frye charts a steadier course, straying not from side to side, but staying rather in the middle of the road. This last phrase now has connotations of a certain bourgeois complacency and conservatism that is foreign to Frye as a matter of principle. Nonetheless one can glimpse a gradual shift from the style and substance of his earlier, more clearly socialist writings to the balanced prose of *The Critical Path.* Frye's position in this later work is more identifiably liberal, and it is no accident that John Stuart Mill is one of the authorities cited in the final phase of the argument. Frye explicitly walks a line between the Scylla and Charbydis of extreme conservative and extreme revolutionary positions, though he continues to call for a critical position, one which remains, almost by definition, off the beaten path.

Toward the end of *The Critical Path* Frye speaks briefly of the university as the institutional locus of criticism, a theme that preoccupies him in a variety of other contexts. Frye was acquainted firsthand with the duties and responsibilities of administrative posts, serving as Principal and Chancellor of Victoria College, as well as on a number of governmental committees. Victoria College at the University of Toronto is a stone's throw from the Ontario Parliament Buildings, the physical proximity being a graphically concrete symbol for the necessarily close relation of government and university in Canadian society. The two institutions of government and university, Frye once contended in a speech honoring John Diefenbaker (then Prime Minister of Canada), are essential to the same society. But, he continued, "there is a natural tension" between them, for the principle of government is majority rule whereas the universities are an effective instrument for the preservation of minority right. "The university," Frye claims, "seeks truth at all cost; the government seeks compromise at all cost."[23] Unlike many universities in the United States, most universities in Canada and Europe are funded in large measure by national, state, or provincial governments, which means that the university's search for truth is caught up in the government's practice of compromise. Ideally, the university remains autonomous with respect to state government, especially in matters of academic freedom. This relative autonomy with respect to government and to society generally is one reason behind the myth of the academic ivory tower, myth here being understood for once in the sense of illusion. What Frye thinks of this notion of the academy is clear from his rhetorical turning of the tables in an address to a convocation of graduating students. He congratulates those students

on "leaving the real world of the university and going out to the confused illusions of the world outside. Soon you will be in the ivory
towers of business, in the escapist retreats of the suburbs, in the charm-
less magic of teaching, or in the schizophrenic fantasies of government."[24] Even if the tone here is somewhat ironic, the statement is
consonant with Frye's view of the university as one locus in society
where criticism and imagination can be set free, left to the disciplining
of their own devices.

The first version of what was to become the "Polemical Introduction" of the *Anatomy* was called "The Function of Criticism at the Present Time," a phrase which cites the title of Matthew Arnold's famous
essay. That same title has been echoed many times since by critics of
various persuasions: essays in this virtual subgenre of criticism tend to
be programmatic and utopian, often bearing the character of a manifesto. As the later title for the essay suggests, there is something explicitly or implicitly polemical about such programs, as they define
themselves against the dominant trends and tendencies of the time.
But the departure of the title of the present chapter ("The Function of
Criticism at Any Given Time") from this tradition points to an aspect
of Frye's work that is precisely opposed to attention to the simply "contemporary" function of criticism. We saw at the end of the *Fearful
Symmetry* that the seemingly archaic practice of Elizabethan critics
"with their rhetorical textbooks and their mythological handbooks"
was held up as exemplary for critical practice.[25] And at the end of the
Anatomy, which proposed to survey all the possible and desirable critical methods, archetypal criticism was privileged as the mode that was
to "supplement" the other existing ones. So too in *The Critical Path*
and numerous essays on the relations of literature and society, Frye
departs from what he calls a "quasi-historical" procedure to speak of a
criticism not limited by its particular historical determinations. He can
write, for example: "It is the critic's task, in every age, to fight for the
autonomy of the arts, and never under any circumstance allow himself
to be seduced into judging the arts, positively or negatively, by their
attachments."[26] One does not need to appeal to phrases like "in every
age" to recognize that Frye proposes that the task of criticism be essentially descriptive and analytic, not judgmental. At some fundamental
level, criticism will always say the same thing, in part because any text
under scrutiny is always saying the same thing. As Frye claims toward
the end of *The Critical Path:* "The document is the model of all teaching, because it is infinitely patient, repeating the same words however

often one consults it, and the spatial focus it provides makes it possible
to return on the experience, a repetition of the kind that underlies all
genuine education" (*CP,* 150). I alluded above to Frye's observation
that the political philosopher writing of utopia was in fact writing
about the theory of education. The reverse is also the case, for the
theory of education always implies a theory of society.[27] And the object
of social criticism, for Frye, is not the ceaseless flux of social configu-
rations and historical action but, paradoxically, the "stable and permanent form" of society.[28] One should not be misled by the seemingly
Platonic rhetoric of "permanent form." As is clear from his study of
Blake, as well as his allegiance to Aristotle, "form" is a category that
can accommodate change within it. Frye clarifies his notion of permanent form in this way: "I mean that genuine society preserves the
continuity of the dead, the living and the unborn, the memory of the
past, the reality of the present, and the anticipation of the future which
is the one unbreakable social contract."[29] Ideally, then, criticism should
always have the same relation to the society in which it functions. But
this is not to say that criticism is somehow transcendental or even
trans-historical. The tasks of reading and writing are for the literary
always to come extend pragmatic and specific, varying from text to
text, which guarantees that criticism will always be "different." To
speak of criticism "at the present time" or "at any given time" is in
the end not very different, if one recognizes that for criticism there is,
as it were, no time like the present.

Chapter Five
Reviewing Canada

It is one of the unspoken ironies of cultural life in Canada that it produced a great critic before a great "writer." Though this proposition is arguable in a number of respects—the distinction between critic and writer is an unstable one—it does point to some of the recurrent problems in the task of Canadian cultural criticism. Not everyone would put Frye in a class above the best "creative" writers of his generation or any previous one. Frye himself would surely deny such a claim, and one hesitates to draw many conclusions from this singular state of affairs. But even the false problem of the opposition between the "creative" writer and the "parasitic" critic suggests some real issues at the center of Canadian culture and its self-understanding. What seems a preposterous state of affairs—that criticism should, in some sense, take "priority" over primary literature—aggravates a near nation-wide neurosis: Canada's preoccupation with its own "identity" and the quality of its artistic production.

One cannot and should not argue on the basis of Frye's unique position that criticism is somehow "prior" to literature in Canadian intellectual life. Historically speaking, literature is fundamental to Canadian life in a way that criticism is not. Even in those areas of Canada where the oppressiveness of nature would seem to make culture a low priority, poetry emerges as much more than ornamental or superfluous. In reviewing a collection of Eskimo poetry, Frye remarks on the difficulty most Canadians (who live in the quasi-temperate zone just north of the American border) have in imagining a life so dominated by a struggle for survival. "What is still more difficult to imagine," Frye continues, "is that when life is reduced to its barest essentials of survival, poetry should turn out to be one of those essentials."[1] Literary criticism, of course, is hardly one of the bare essentials on the order of the poetic myths the Eskimos created for themselves. But as we saw in the last chapter, a literary culture cannot function for very long without something like "criticism." Not that this criticism need take its now familiar institutionalized and academic forms, but at least some considered response to artistic production appears crucial to society at large, not just to a specialized class of literati.

Within Canada, Frye's preeminence as a critic has much to do with the authority of his writings on his own country's culture, a corpus virtually unknown outside Canada, even to many of those who have written at length on other aspects of his work. We saw in the chapter on romance that Frye's "predilection" for romance and comedy, his persona as an *"Odyssey"* critic, turned out to have important implications for his literary theory as a whole. So too does his work on Canadian culture qualify and complicate (for his readers) the rest of his oeuvre, because it forces reconsideration of many sides of his work, especially with regard to the status of history and the role of regionalism in cultural production. In speaking of the Olympian perspective achieved in Frye's *Anatomy of Criticism,* Geoffrey Hartman rightly remarked that it would be reductive to think of Frye as "a Canadian summing up Canadian experience," yet Frye can with good reason contend that even his work on world literature "has always been rooted in Canada and drawn its essential characteristics from there" (*BG,* i).[2]

It is not a matter of indifference that so many of Frye's writings on Canadian culture take the form of the review. Frye's earliest published writings were for the most part reviews contributed to the *Canadian Forum,* and he singles out his review of A. J. M. Smith's *Book of Canadian Poetry* as his "first critical article of any lasting importance" (*BG,* vii). His most significant contribution to Canadian letters, at least in terms of the somewhat elusive phenomenon of influence, was the annual review of poetry in Canada featured in the *University of Toronto Quarterly* from 1950 to 1959. The review as a genre makes special demands on the critic at the same time that it presents special possibilities, particularly for a kind of writing distinct from that of the scholarly article or book. In the *Anatomy* (much of which was composed during the same period as the columns on poetry for the *University of Toronto Quarterly*), Frye had argued that evaluation could play no role in the development of a scientific criticism. Not that evaluation was to be banished from the domain of criticism altogether: Frye simply wanted to distinguish as clearly as possible between analytic issues of structure, myth, and the like on the one hand, and taste on the other. On these grounds, it has to be acknowledged that much of Frye's writing on Canadian literature cannot be termed "scientific." While evaluation is by no means the goal of Frye's Canadian criticism, its role here, almost by virtue of the review form alone, is much more prominent than in his other work. In a review, one concern for writer and reader is the simple pragmatic judgment as to whether or not a book in question is "worth" reading. This too is in theory something of a false issue, since Frye agrees with Milton in his *Areopagitica* that a wise man can make good use of a bad book just as a fool may abuse the Bible. But the pragmatic question of evaluation will never quite go away, and Frye follows the dictates of the genre in being, among other things, an arbiter of taste. Thus he will applaud Irving Layton for "telling the whole disinterested imaginative truth about his subject, free of both querulousness and posing" (*BG,* 69) or, in more conventional reviewer's prose, comment that Patrick Anderson's *The Color as Naked* is "delightful to read and is recommended without reservation" (*BG,* 24). Neither will he hesitate to pronounce a whole year's poetic production "unusually thin" (*BG,* 70). Evaluation may not be a part of scientific criticism, but it certainly finds its place in Frye's Canadian writings.

Frye has been a champion of Canadian letters, especially at a time when Canada had not quite decided whether it deserved a champion. Though Frye's reading of the corpus of his country's literature is not at all clouded by blind faith in Canadiana, he does tend to give poets the benefit of the doubt, and the result is a generous, expansive vision of the achievement and potential of Canadian poetry. His writings on Canadian literature are considerably more evaluative than his other texts, but he still contends, from within the former body of work, that evaluation is a peripheral concern for criticism. Indeed, Frye can write in the conclusion to the first edition of *A Literary History of Canada* that "to study Canadian literature properly, one must outgrow the view that evaluation is the end of criticism, instead of its incidental by-product" (*BG,* 213). Yet the task of evaluation is one of the occupational hazards of being a *Canadian* critic: "The critic of Canadian literature has to settle uneasily somewhere between the Canadian historian or social scientist, who has no comparative value-judgements to worry about, and the ordinary literary critic, who has nothing else" (*BG,* 163). Here Frye is commenting on the special importance of a nation's literature for its sense of identity. Canadian literature is important for Canadians to read, quite apart from any considerations of its quality, simply because literature affords a way of "getting one's bearings." The task of Canadian cultural criticism is hardly seized by Frye as an opportunity to wallow, self-indulgently, in "Canadiana." In most respects, Canadian literature must be read as any other corpus: as

Frye has said on several occasions, "the ultimate standards of Canadian literature have to be international ones."[3]

For whom is a review written? Not for the poets, Frye claims. "The reviewer," he contends:

> knows that he will be read by poets, but he is not addressing them, except indirectly. It is no part of the reviewer's task to tell the poet how to write or how he should have written. The one kind of criticism that the poet himself, *qua* poet, engages in—the technical self-criticism which leads to revision and improvement—is a criticism with which the reviewer has nothing to do. Nor is it his task to encourage or discourage poets. . . . The reviewer's audience is the community of actual and potential readers of poetry. His task is to show what is available in poetic experience, to suggest that reading is an essential cultural activity. . . . He has the special problem, too, of bridging the gap between poetry and its public. . . .
>
> (*BG*, 124–25)

The reviewer, then, is not responsible for policing the production of literature. He or she is much more concerned with the reading and understanding of poetry, taking an active part in unleashing its imaginative force for society at large. The reading of poetry, of which reviewing is only one institutionalized form, is best not regarded as a pastime to be taken up at one's leisure. In reading and reviewing begin responsibilities.

Still another formal feature of the review as a genre requires some attention here: the implicit impetus it affords for re-vision. A scholarly article is designed to have a lengthy shelf-life, to be read whenever a reader's subject matter demands it, so to speak. But the review in a journal or quarterly is a much more ephemeral thing, usually inscribed with a greater sense of urgency and topicality. The text or texts under consideration present the occasion for a re-view of the current state of affairs and a prospect for the future. The review typically asks two implicit questions: "What has been done?" and "What is to be done?" This visionary or re-visionary character carries over into many of Frye's writings that are not strictly speaking reviews, though they resemble works of that genre more than they do scholarly articles. A number of Frye's major statements on Canadian culture take the form of introductions or conclusions to large-scale, collaborative projects like the several editions of *A Literary History of Canada*. And if a suitably comprehensive book does not exist to review reviewing, Frye does not hesitate to invent it, as he does in the fanciful "Preface to an Uncollected Anthology." In this last piece, the utopian impulse in Frye is particularly clear, and it demonstrates how a certain visionary mode inhabits Frye's criticism as much as the literature on which he comments.

The curious "primacy" of Frye as a critic over the majority of authors in the world of Canadian letters has something to do with the fact that he was the teacher of a good many of them, including Margaret Atwood, Dennis Lee, Margaret Avison, and James Reaney, to name but a few. Frye vigorously denies that there is such a thing as a "Northrop Frye school of poetry," but there is no denying that he helped teach a generation of poets, directly and indirectly, to read.[4] And since poems come from other poems, a poet's "reading" of the tradition is a driving force behind poetic production. Certainly, Canadian poetry of the last few decades is markedly mythopoeic, often in a self-conscious way, and some part of this movement can be ascribed to Frye's influence.[5]

Another current of Frye's work that surfaces in his writings on Canadian culture is an almost singular emphasis on thematics, in the common sense of the term (as opposed to the way "thematic" is defined in the *Anatomy*). This too goes against the grain of Frye's other work, as he practices something different from what the *Anatomy* preaches. Again this has something to do with the specific determination of the genre of the review, but even more to do with the history of Canadian criticism, or rather the lack of it, before Frye. Just as evaluation is something eventually to be outgrown, so thematic criticism seems more appropriate, indeed excusable, in a nascent period of criticism. Questions of what literature is "about" almost always take historical priority over questions of "how" literature goes about it. Thus it seems more appropriate for criticism to start out with thematic concerns such as nature, survival, or communication than with investigations of more purely formal features of literary texts.[6] There is of course often a fine line between archetypal and thematic criticism; how nature is represented in a literary text, for example, is equally the province of both approaches. And here too the question of the review as genre comes into play, since the brief, semipopular form of the review is less conducive to formalist analysis than to a preliminary orientation into and assessment of the text.

Another curious feature of the corpus of Frye's writings on Canada is the virtual absence of a reflection on drama. The explanation for this "neglect" is at least partially accounted for by Frye's analysis of the historical conditions of drama's impossibility in Canada: "Certain features of life in a new country that are bound to handicap its writers are obvious enough. In drama, which depends on a theatre and consequently on a highly organized urban life, the foreshortening of historical development has been particularly cruel, as drama was strangled by the movie just as it was getting started as a popular medium" (*BG*, 222). That statement, written in the 1960s, looks back on the whole sweep of Canadian drama, or what there was of it.[7] Frye is more sanguine about the state of Canadian theater in 1977 when he reviews the impact of the Stratford festival, devoted primarily to the work of Shakespeare, who was not, it should go without saying, a Canadian dramatist. But only the most xenophobic of nationalists would decry the influence the festival had. As Frye notes: "it helped to foster a school of Canadian actors, and the lift in morale it represented fostered Canadian playwriting as well."[8] Both of these judgments on the theater belong more to the sphere of cultural history than to the scientific discipline of literary criticism as outlined in the *Anatomy*. There is little criticism of individual plays or even of trends in Canadian drama in Frye, and this absence of any sustained reflection on drama contributes to the emphasis on thematics in his Canadian criticism. It is above all in Frye's work on drama, especially Shakespearean drama, that the insistence on issues of structure is most pronounced. In short, drama precludes through its formal properties attention to a lyric or narrative voice, the seductive presence of which often leads to thematic criticism.

What then are the themes that dominate Frye's Canadian writings, the presence of which has occasioned the objections of a number of critics?[9] The obvious starting point is not of Frye's choosing. One could not get very far in Canadian intellectual life of the past three or four decades without encountering the ubiquitous anxiety about the national "identity." If that obsession has abated now, it is partly out of sheer tedium, and because in many respects it emerged as an immense false problem. With the flowering of the literary "bush garden" in those same years, it finally registered on the Canadian consciousness that whatever happens in Canada is Canadian. This fact has always been true but is more readily recognized when the notion of what is Canadian coincides with the notion of what is good. Already in 1943 in his important review of A. J. M. Smith's *Book of Canadian Poetry*, Frye could write: "Now admittedly a great deal of useless yammering has been concerned with the truly Canadian qualities of our literature, and one's first instinct is to avoid the whole question" (*BG*, 131). The endeavor of finding out what is "truly Canadian" is often part of a program to establish normative standards by which much of what is necessarily Canadian could be disregarded as not "truly" so. A policing of what is *echt* Canadian is hardly the most productive way to further Canadian culture. Regardless of the success of this policing of the Canadian or of a resistance to that tendency, there are historical and linguistic forces at work that form something unique and untranslatable: "no one who knows the country will deny that there is something, say an attitude of mind, distinctively Canadian, and while Canadian speech is American, there is a recognizable Canadian accent in the more highly organized speech of its poetry" (*BG,* 131). There is of course no such thing as a "distinctively Canadian language": the poet "is compelled to take the language he was brought up to speak, whether French, English, or Icelandic, and attempt to adjust that language to an environment which is foreign to it, if not foreign to himself" (*BG,* 145). So the critic has to walk a fine line between what is and is not peculiarly Canadian: any study in Canadian literature will necessarily be an exercise in "comparative literature," for whatever the Canadian is, its identity is constituted in terms of what it is not.[10]

What then of Canadian writers' relation to their "own" tradition? One of the more productive trends in contemporary literary criticism has addressed the topic called alternately "the burden of the past" or "the anxiety of influence."[11] When Frye comes to discuss patterns of imagery in Canadian poetry, his essay on the topic is entitled "Haunted by a Lack of Ghosts," a phrase adapted from the closing lines of a poem by Earle Birney called "Can. Lit." Frye does not dwell on the darker aspects of Birney's poetical comment on Canadian literary history, choosing instead to focus on the relation of man to nature. He observes by way of introduction to his title that "there is a lurking feeling that if anything did speak to the poet from nature it would speak only to condemn."[12] But one thing to which the "lack of ghosts" in Birney's poem refers is the absence of an indigenous tradition of literary models. This literary history without a history has divergent repercussions. On the one hand, there is considerable anxiety to produce chimeras like "the great Canadian novel." On the other hand, the Canadian writer need not look over his or her shoulder the way that, say, a British poet of the eighteenth century would in the wake of Milton. For the psyche of the Canadian writer, the absence of a "great tradition" can be debilitating, enabling, or both.

The other great thematic concern of Frye's Canadian criticism is nature, the intractable fact of Canadian life in an age when the environment is threatened with obliteration. For a time, nature and culture seemed to combine in making Canada a habitat for the pastoral mode: Wordsworth and the woods, one could say, were the twin muses of Canadian poetry in the nineteenth century. Nature in the vast expanses of Canada varies wildly from region to region. And the poetic environment is shaded variously in accordance with regional differences: Frye can even discern an alliance between the Newfoundland setting of E. J. Pratt's poetry and the elegiac form he adopts. Gradually the dichotomy of man and nature that marks the eighteenth and nineteenth centuries in Canada (or perhaps just the seventeenth and nineteenth: Frye says in one place that "Canada had no eighteenth century") is displaced by the "triangular conflict of nature, society, and individual" (*BG*, 245). Nature tends to get absorbed, as far as possible, as an aspect of culture. But when called upon to characterize the quintessence of Canadian literature, Frye reasserts nature itself as the primary category: "everything that is central in Canadian writing seems to be marked by the imminence of the natural world. The sense of this imminence organizes the mythology of Jay Macpherson; it is the sign in which Canadian soldiers conquer Italy in Douglas LePan's *The Net and the Sword;* it may be in the foreground, as in Alden Nowlan, or in the background, as in Birney; but it is always there" (*BG*, 247).

Nature may well be the force that most binds Canadians together. Nations, by Frye's reckoning, thrive on having something of which to be proud and something to fear: nature serves both these functions in Canada. But as man gradually comes to terms with nature, those terms are caught up in social concerns that for the most part leave nature behind. Having first identified nature, Canada must then somehow identify itself. The determination of Canadian identity—even if one is to conclude that there is no such thing—cannot proceed for very long without considering how other national and linguistic constituencies inform Canada's own. The vast territory that is now Canada was the site of struggle between the colonial powers England and France, and the uneasy accord between English and French—that Frye calls "a more or less amiable apartheid"—continues to this day. The United States was similarly the site of colonial struggle, but the outcome of that struggle had one major and far-reaching difference. The American colonies established their independence through a revolution, and a good many of the Loyalists came to settle in Canada where an antirevolutionary, not to say counterrevolutionary, tendency has reigned ever since. Hence the Canadian radical turns out, typically, to be that odd hybrid, the "Tory radical." The principal consequence of the absence of a Canadian Revolution is that the country has remained much more of a colony in fact and in spirit. In the preface to *The Bush Garden,* Frye could still claim, as late as 1971, that Canada was "practically the only country left in the world which is a pure colony, colonial in psychology as well as in mercantile economics" (*BG,* iii). No sooner had Canada ceased to be a British colony than it became, in effect, something of an American one, for in the course of the twentieth century Canada's economy became inextricably bound up in that of its larger, richer, and more imperial neighbor. Canada's fate seemed, once again, to be in the hands of others. In the decades of Frye's most concentrated attention to matters of Canadian culture—roughly from the end of World War II to the mid-sixties—the American media, especially television, threatened to overwhelm their Canadian counterparts to the point of provoking a powerful wave of anti-American sentiment. At its worst, this led to xenophobia and jingoism; at its best, it pointed to some more genuine issues of Canadian self-determination. Throughout this period, one tends to think of Canada as a "nation," almost by definition. But Frye maintains that Canada in fact has gone through periods of being a pre-nation and a post-nation "without ever having become a nation."[13] By the time Canada began to lose some of its colonial character, it was already caught up in the larger historical forces of industrial and multinational capitalism, for which the notion of a nation is necessarily anachronistic. One cannot appeal any longer to the foreshortened history of Canada by speaking of it as a "young country," for it is precisely the same age as any other country at a similarly advanced stage of capitalist development.[14]

To consider culture primarily under the rubric of the "nation" is to obscure many matters from the outset. One risks not seeing the trees for the forest, so to speak. This, at least, is Frye's later view of the importance of the regional environment for cultural production. In his early review of Smith's *The Book of Canadian Poetry,* Frye had claimed that culture seems to flourish best in national units, "which implies that the empire is too big and the province too small for major literature" (*BG,* 133). Together with the imperial, Frye names the regional as "an inherently anti-poetic environment" and the two make up what he calls "the colonial" in Canadian life (*BG,* 133). In his later work, however, the "region" has become the privileged locus of cultural creativity. Thus in a paper titled "Culture as Interpenetration" (1977) Frye can claim:

The general principle appears to be that a painter or writer who is self-conscious about his immediate context will be likely to sound provincial, whereas a painter or writer who accepts a provincial milieu in, say, Newfoundland or southern British Columbia, will be much less likely to do so. . . . Within the last twenty years we have been seeing more and more areas of this huge and sparsely settled country become culturally visible through painters and writers who belong, as creative people, less to Canada than to the Prairies, the Pacific coast, the Atlantic coast, southern Ontario or Quebec.[15]

Though the second passage on regionalism appears revisionary of the first, there is in fact no contradiction between the two, since in Frye's view there has been a historical change in the relation between regional and national culture within Canada. In his earliest writings Frye took pains to point out the vigorously regional dimensions of Canadian politics, with the separatist movement in Quebec being only the most visible and violent. But in the sixties especially, with the period of Canada's literary "explosion"—as Frye terms it—culture began to pull in the opposite direction of a unifying movement in politics.[16] Canadian culture now shifted increasingly toward regional diversification, and this movement was no longer "provincial" in the pejorative sense. Indeed, it marked a shift from "inarticulate form to articulate content."[17]

   In searching for a way to characterize the attitude particular to Canadian culture, Frye found it helpful to think in terms of Canada's "garrison mentality" (*BG*, 236). Canada's colonial history began, of course, with literal garrisons being cornerstones of society. But the metaphor remains appropriate long after the original referent has disappeared. "A garrison," Frye writes, "is a closely knit and beleaguered society, and its moral and social values are unquestionable" (*BG*, 226). Even the largest of Canadian centers retains something of the garrison mentality because each is "confronted with a huge, unthinking, menacing, and formidable physical setting" (*BG*, 225). Frye finds that a "terror of nature" runs all through Canadian literature, but a terror less of the actual dangers of nature than of its "unconsciousness," that which is utterly alien to human consciousness. Such an environment, physical or otherwise, is conducive to popular literature with strongly defined ethical positions, as with the black and white characters of romance and melodrama, for example. The literature produced will be rather more rhetorical than poetic, a rhetoric which Frye characterizes as "using language as one would use an axe" (*BG*, 228). The transition from rhetoric (the impulse to assert) to poetics (the impulse to construct) is accomplished gradually, a movement that accompanies the transition "from the fortress to the metropolis" (*BG*, 231).

To speak of "the garrison mentality" in the singular is somewhat misleading, if it is thought to imply too great a degree of homogeneity. One reason that the question of Canadian identity emerges as a false problem is that there has been a marked heterogeneity from the very beginning of the country's history, with its uneasy co-presence of English Protestant and French Catholics.[18] When one further takes into consideration the pre-colonial indigenous peoples, as well as the wide spectrum of immigrants, one realizes how utterly fictitious any notion of the typical Canadian would be. It is with good reason that Canadians have long felt that the appropriate metaphor for the constitution of their society was not the melting pot but the mosaic.

The considerable body of Frye's work on Canadian culture remains largely unread outside his own country, though that may well change as the cycles of taste in criticism circle back to rediscover his writings time and time again: they anticipate, for example, much current work on the theory and the practice of "minor literature." Taken together, Frye's reviews, introductions, afterwords, and essays form a remarkable running commentary on the period in which Canadian literature finally came of age. And when considered in the light of his total oeuvre, theoretical and practical, the writings on Canadian culture clarify and expand a vision of literature whose quest for form is always the same and always different, subject to the mythical and generic determinations of literature, as well as to the irreducibly variegated environments in which poets live and work, read and write.

Chapter Six
The Great Coda:
The Bible and Literature

It is no wonder that with his last grand project, *The Great Code: The Bible and Literature*, Frye's itinerary should come full circle. His principal contribution in *Fearful Symmetry* had been to render intelligible the difficult poetry of William Blake by reading it in its proper mythological context, primarily that of the Bible. Blake was seen as exemplary of the mythopoeic mind at work, as a poet for whom the Bible was much more than "background." In *The Great Code*, from the title of the text onwards, Blake is still a guiding spirit, but this time the Bible itself takes center stage, "a huge, sprawling, tactless book" standing in "the middle of our cultural heritage."[1]

The Great Code is designed as a book for the general reader: it makes no pretensions to be a contribution to the scholarly study of the Bible, though every biblical scholar would do well to read it. Frye's study was not greeted with the same level of praise lavished on *Fearful Symmetry* or the *Anatomy*, though this may have less to do with the quality of the text than its sometimes disconcerting tone and content.[2] *The Great Code* is one of Frye's most challenging books, despite its popular, nonscholarly character. It offers one of the most sustained and profound attempts to address the language and structure of the Bible from a perspective that is fundamentally nondoctrinal.

In his introduction, Frye is almost disingenuous in calling attention to the book's status as a personal statement. The near-tautology of the phrasing "my own personal encounter with the Bible" is rare in Frye, for stylistic and other reasons. Part of the distinctive character of the undertaking can be ascribed to Frye's avowed attempt to read the Bible "from the point of view of a literary critic" (*GC*, xi). At the outset Frye wants to distinguish what he is doing from those who think in terms of the "Bible as literature" and teach courses under that rubric. Rather than reading the Bible as an anthology of Near Eastern literature, Frye wants to grapple with the text as the tenuous unity that it is. For reasons distinct from those of the so-called higher critics, he

wants to know why the Bible is structured in the canonical form that
has come down to us. Frye is content to leave the sifting of the many
layers of the biblical palimpsest to textual scholars.[3] Yet despite the
apology for a simply "personal" view of the Bible, the present task still
belongs to the larger project of scientific criticism, for which the *Anatomy of Criticism* laid the theoretical foundation.

The *Great Code* grows out of Frye's teaching for many years in a
course on the mythological framework of Western literature. He notes
that in his experience of teaching the Bible the material could often be
"emotionally explosive." The simple division of the Bible into Old and
New Testaments marks the history of divisive conflicts that go well
beyond matters of textual interpretation. Can the choice to focus on
the Christian Bible be a harmless decision? No: the decision depends
in part on what Frye elsewhere calls mythological or ideological conditioning. This sets limits for, but does not disqualify the possibility
of, a "scientific," that is to say "systematic" or "coherent," study of the
Bible in terms of literary criticism.

I noted in the *Anatomy of Criticism* a somewhat mysterious appeal to
"the order of words" as a foundation for the scientific study of literature. The phrase reappears as the title for the first of the two halves of
The Great Code, where it is much clearer what Frye has in mind. The
text begins with nothing less than a theory and a history of language
within which the Bible may be considered. Once again, Vico is a kind
of Virgilian guide through the tangled history of the West, for his *New
Science* offers a typological and historical model to account for three
modes of language that have dominated the cyclical movements of
Western culture.

Vico is appropriate for Frye's concerns in part because he realized
that in the beginning was the poetic word. Frye is eminently attentive
to the way the Bible, like most sacred books, is written with "the
concentration of poetry" (*GC,* 3). One enormous complication for
Christians is that, almost from the beginning, they were fated to read
this divine poetry in translation. Even the authors of the New Testament write in a koine Greek that is not their native language. Translation, like necessity, is a mother of invention, but it is only possible
if one posits beyond the particular *langue* (or individual tongue) some
langage (language in general) that would be the common ground of
sense to which any specific *langue* could be referred.[4] But even this
more encompassing, universal *langage* has a certain history of its own,
and Vico is one of its shrewdest historians.

For Vico there were three ages in the cycle of history, which Frye outlines as follows: "a mythical age, or age of gods; a heroic age, or age of an aristocracy; and an age of the people, after which there comes a *ricorso* or return that starts the whole process over again. Each age produces its own kind of *langage,* giving us three types of verbal expression that Vico calls, respectively, the poetic, the heroic or noble, and the vulgar, and which I shall call the hieroglyphic, the hieratic, and the demotic" (*GC,* 5). In the first age, of which Homer is an exemplar, language is poetic and concrete.[5] It could also be described as "metaphorical," though that term itself only arises in the second phase of language. What we would usually consider metaphors in Homer are not yet metaphors because they are not quite opposed to "proper" meanings. By the time of Plato, words no longer have the "quasi-physical power" (*GC,* 6) of the first phase, but have become "primarily the outward expression of inner thoughts or ideas" (*GC,* 7), with subjects and objects now clearly delineated.[6] If metaphor is (unself-consciously) the characteristic figure of speech in the first phase, metonymy is the paradigm for the second. In Frye's terms, the radical form of metaphor takes the form of "this is that," whereas in metonymy "this is put for that." The second phase is more consonant with the sequential construction of continuous prose than with the discontinuous forms of poetry. These differences in linguistic structure have serious consequences for the Bible and religious language generally. For example, language of the first phase tends to be polytheistic, in contrast to the monotheistic stamp of the second phase. It is not quite accurate to think of the Bible as resolutely monotheistic, for there is an undeniable polytheism to some strains of the Genesis narrative and other Old Testament books.[7]

The third phase of language, Frye observes, "begins roughly in the sixteenth century, where it accompanies certain tendencies in the Renaissance and Reformation, and attains cultural ascendancy in the eighteenth. In English literature it begins theoretically with Francis Bacon, and effectively with Locke" (*GC,* 13). The third phase retains a great deal in common with the second, but it departs in particular from syllogistic reasoning and an analogical view of language. This last phase of the three coincides with the rise of modern science, complete with its emphasis on empirical fact-finding.[8] Language is now prized for its ability to describe the natural order of an objective world, with truth being defined in terms of the correspondence between language and the external order to which it refers.

Most of the Bible is written in the second phase of Vico's (and now Frye's) scheme of language, with echoes of the first and only the faintest of anticipations of the third. Most commentary on the Bible since the seventeenth century falls decidedly into the third phase, which means that it is usually allegorical, as would be any translation from the first phase to the second. Yet even the three comprehensive models of language suggested by Vico are not quite enough to account for the texture of the Bible. Frye turns to Cicero and classical rhetoric for a supplementary paradigm that shares something of the highly figured speech of the first phase and the reasoned argument of the second: namely, oratory. The appeal to oratory is not surprising given the necessity of persuasion: indeed the word "orator" as a translation for the Hebrew *nabi* captures a good deal more than the misleading rendition as "prophet." At the highest level of oracular, exhortatory rhetoric is *kerygma,* meaning proclamation or message, a term that Frye adopts as a fourth form of expression to supplement the three Viconian phases. But it seems that Frye himself proclaims more about *kerygma* than he explains. He can define it only in negative terms ("it is not an argument disguised by figuration") or by translating it ("it is the vehicle of what is traditionally called revelation" [*GC,* 29]), and one is not sure why this linguistic vehicle is not included in the phases previously outlined.

One vehicle of revelation that Frye notes earlier in this introduction to biblical language is something that cannot be comprehended under the rubrics of figurative language, argument, or description. Two examples of this sort of revelation are among the most crucial of divine pronouncements. The first is the celebrated dictum from Exodus "I am that I am," a phrase better translated as "I will be what I will be." In this revised translation, God is less a noun than a verb, specifically a verb that promises something for the future. God not only makes a covenant with the people of Israel, but is Himself already a covenant. A promise is what J. L. Austin calls a performative speech-act, insofar as it does something in the very act of being enunciated, and in this regard the modern notion of the speech-act captures something of the identity of word and event in the Hebrew word *dabar.*[9] Frye's second example from the Old Testament, "God said, Let there be light, and there was light," is also a speech-act, one with a divinely immediate effect. Indeed, one thing that forever separates divine from human speech is that the former always delivers what it promises. In this example, we can also glimpse something of the gulf that separates, in theory, religious from secular literature. We recall from the *Anatomy* that the literary text is a hypothetical verbal construct, but the divine speech act is, ideally, a hypothesis that always turns out to be the case. This emphasis on the performance of language in the Bible anticipates Frye's speculations, here and elsewhere, on the elusive fourth phase of language, which is not entirely a historically discrete one, though it is the twentieth-century philosophers Wittgenstein, Austin, and Derrida who seem to be its foremost theorists. *Kerygma* may not be the best term for this phase, but at the very least it points to the enigmatic complexity of biblical language. For all its schematization, the opening chapter of *The Great Code* does not leave one with a very clear picture of the Bible's language, in part because the language exceeds the limits of any picture. In the *Anatomy*, we noticed the limits of the pictorial or representation model in its attempt to account for "the order of words." In *The Great Code*, the busy canvas of the beginning gives way in the following chapter to what is surely the most remarkable aspect of the Bible: its story.

The first chapter on "language" addressed the structures of language in general, and the turn to "Myth" entails a focus on the specific ordering of words in the Bible. "Myth" retains here its primary sense of narrative or plot, though it is also important as a story or group of stories that are crucial for a given society to know. Still a third sense of "myth"—one virtually banished from Frye's lexicon since the Blake book—as a story that does not correspond to the truth has to be recalled, if only provisionally. Frye firmly rejects the view of Sir James Frazer that myths are "mistaken explanations" of what actually happened.[10] But the question of the mythical status of the Bible cannot be dismissed out of hand because in some traditions the truth claim of the Bible depends in part on its historical reference. The Bible presents much more than a compilation of religious doctrine: it recounts in large measure the history of God and his peoples, Israelites and Christians. But the Bible offers a "violently partisan" view of history: it is, among other things, a massive piece of "propaganda" (*GC,* 40). Frye claims that when one examines stories that have the form of histories, more often than not they turn out to exist for reasons other than those of historical reference. There is little historical evidence for the exodus from Egypt, for example, but the "history" of Israel is hardly conceivable without it. And the Book of Judges is one instance of many in which the events have been carefully edited to create a more unified front.

Lest Frye be suspected here, as a reader with a Christian bias, of being too severe a critic of the Old Testament, it soon becomes clear that the New Testament fares little better on grounds of historical accuracy. The four evangelists, for example, evince little interest or proficiency in biography but are expert in relating the "events" of Jesus' life to the prophecies of the Old Testament. The Gospels display a sure sense of symmetry in themselves and in relation to the Hebrew Scriptures, and "symmetry in any narrative," Frye maintains, "always means that historical content is being subordinated to mythical demands of design and form" (GC, 43).[11] A "literal" understanding of the Bible—that is, one that identifies the literal sense as the historical—turns out to be precisely the wrong approach to take in reading the Scriptures.[12] The Bible, much like sublime poetry in Blake's dictum, is allegory addressed to the intellectual powers.

Whatever the vagaries of its historical reference, the Bible has a powerful function in society that transcends questions of truth and falsity. The Bible cannot be reduced to the merely hypothetical basis of poetry, in which case it would appear as a "spectacularly bad . . . poem" (GC, 47). It functions as the basis for interpretation and action in the world, and at the same time intimates something beyond that world. When we read the words of the black spiritual "Go down, Moses, / Way down in Egypt land, / Tell old Pharaoh / Let my people go," the verses have little to do with any actual Egypt, past or present. But they sound a rallying cry that points from *Weltgeschichte* (world history) to *Heilsgeschichte* (salvation history). The Bible, in short, is ultimately more important for what it enables than for what it describes.

Frye's elegant and erudite critique of the Bible as a repository of historical truths does much to show the Scripture's identity with and difference from poetry. But his discussion leaves unexplored lingering questions about the Bible's truth in any revisionary, nonreferential sense. If the Bible is not even an oblique account of what really happened, what reason is there to value it over any other sacred text? Christianity is not the only faith grounded in a historical revelation, and surely not all such revelations are created equal. Much as Frye relegates evaluation to a realm outside the sphere of criticism, he prefers here simply to describe and analyze scriptural texts, not to evaluate them. Frye is to an extraordinary degree able to keep separate his faith as a Christian and his insights as a critic. Many "believers" will be disconcerted to read in Frye's pages that Israel was as "cruel and ruthless" a nation as Egypt or that Israel was "unlucky at the game of empire." When treating textual matters, Frye the anatomist takes precedence over Frye the ideologue.[13]

The Bible may not be simply literary in intent or function, but it exhibits all of literature's characteristics and more. When one moves from the overarching constructions of myth to the more intricate workings of words and phrases, one encounters all the tropes and figures traditionally associated with poetic speech. This should come as no surprise to the reader, and Frye's rehearsal of this observation is not new. More distinctive in Frye's argument in the third chapter, "Metaphor I," is the contention that metaphor surpasses the function of "incidental ornament" to count as "one of its controlling modes of thought" (*GC*, 54).[14] Indeed, metaphor pervades the most elemental aspects of Christian faith. As Frye observes: "The sense in Christianity of a faith beyond reason, which must continue to affirm even after reason gives up, is closely connected with the linguistic fact that many of the central doctrines of traditional Christianity can be grammatically expressed only in the form of metaphor. Thus: Christ *is* God and man; in the Trinity three persons *are* one; in the Real Presence the body and blood *are* the bread and the wine" (*GC*, 55). Metaphor takes up, in the Christian reading of the Old Testament, a central theological and hermeneutic position, for the whole notion of "spiritual" interpretation, linked as it is to the Holy Spirit, is inseparable from reading metaphorically. Spiritual or metaphorical understanding of Scripture is only superficially opposed to "literal" understanding. The latter should mean, in Frye's view, any interpretation that takes words seriously, for which there will always be an interplay between metaphorical and literal senses, quite unlike literal interpretation among fundamentalists who would not recognize an allegory if they stumbled over one. One of Frye's chief contributions here, as in the *Anatomy* and elsewhere, is to display the considerable range in kinds of metaphor, from explicit to implicit. The examples of radical or explicit metaphor just cited are quite different in form and function from the sort of metaphorical exchange that occurs in the simple juxtaposition of words, in the way a word is defined by its placement among other words. Juxtaposition is as much a matter of metonymy as metaphor, but Frye insists that the unity of the Bible is not primarily "a metonymic consistency of doctrine addressed to our faith: it is a unity of narrative and imagery and what we have called implicit metaphor" (*GC*, 62).

Even when one acknowledges that Frye is writing of the Bible as a literary critic, it is difficult to overestimate the importance Frye assigns to words. In commenting on the extravagance of the Bible's metaphorical texture and the impossibility of referential reading, Frye can speculate: "We could almost say that even the existence of God is an inference from the existence of the Bible: in the *beginning* was the Word" (*GC*, 61). With the qualification of "almost" Frye refrains from committing himself entirely to one position or the other, but the sentence does proceed to say in a provocative way precisely what could only "almost" be said. This improbable possibility lingers in the reader's mind, and it is this sort of rhetoric that disturbed the book's earliest commentators. But Frye picks up where this doubt leaves off, now in a better position to argue for his resolutely logocentric vision of the Christian religion. What the word of God reveals, for Frye, is the *word* of God, and it is the genius of the Christian Bible to have identified, in the first place, "word" and "God" in the single metaphor of the Logos.

The metaphorical structure of the Bible follows the same principles as do all literary symbols in the manner outlined in the *Anatomy:* Biblical symbols too are organized both dialectically (heaven versus hell, for example) and cyclically, according to the rhythms of nature. But it is the emphasis on the importance of the Word that prevents the mythical organization of metaphor from being simply assimilated to nature. The myth of the Bible is remarkable for its insistence on a total beginning and a total end to time and space, with both beginning and end depending entirely on God's word.

To this point in *The Great Code,* the Bible has emerged as a text much like any other to have been probed by Frye's anatomical instruments. But with the final chapter of Part One, the reader arrives at an issue that is unique to the Bible: namely, typology. Before the New Testament took shape, Scripture was identified with what was eventually to be called, polemically, the Old Testament. The New Testament begins with a reading of the Old; indeed, the "history" presented in the Gospels seems at every turn to be filtered through the text of the Hebrew Scriptures. This structure offers difficulties for any attempt to prove the truth of the Gospels *or* the Old Testament prophecies. Frye says of the two testaments that they "form a double mirror, each reflecting the other but neither the world outside" (*GC*, 78).[15]

The New Testament, then, is self-consciously presented as the "key" to the Old. Everything of moment in the later Testament appears as the "antitype"—the word is Saint Paul's—for its corresponding "type" in the Hebrew Scriptures, as Adam is a "type" for the "antitype" of Christ. Relations of this sort pervade the Bible, so much so that Frye can claim "no other book in the world, to my knowledge, has a structure even remotely like that of the Christian Bible" (*GC*, 80). At one level, typology is simply a figure of speech: Adam resembles Christ in certain respects and can be seen as a figure for him. But typology is as much a mode of thought as it is a figure of speech. It structures numerous movements of the Bible—for typology is a figure that unites two or more moments in time—and indeed comes to inform the way history is experienced within the biblical period.

Typology is, in its very structure, forward-looking and thus particularly well-suited to the demands of early Christianity, which needed to preserve an identity with the Hebrew tradition at the same time that it distanced itself from that tradition. But typology is by no means merely a Christian "invention," for it is already at work within the Hebrew Scriptures themselves. "The most important single historical fact about the Old Testament," Frye notes in iconoclastic fashion, "is that the people who produced it were never lucky at the game of empire" (*GC*, 83). Thus their historical gaze was directed toward the future, to the coming of the Messiah and the restoration of Israel. In the transition from Old to New Testaments, one of the many changes is the shift in emphasis from the society of Israel to the person of Jesus. Part of this shift is prepared for by what Frye calls the "royal metaphor," whereby an individual is identified "with" and "as" the class or body he or she represents, as a king is identified with and as his people.[16] The typological structure and texture of the Bible clearly leaves much "room for interpretation," since the connections between types and antitypes can depend to some extent on the ingenuity of the reader. A highly typological and highly figurative text like the Book of Revelation left, in Frye's words, "commentators on it free to identify its sinister images of Antichrist and Great Whore with whatever they were most afraid of in their day" (*GC*, 95).[17]

The pressure toward the apocalyptic in the Christian tradition contrasts starkly with the great classical poems contemporary with early Christian society, Virgil's *Aeneid* and Ovid's *Metamorphoses*. The action of these pagan poems offers dim analogues to corresponding parts of the Bible, but the decisive difference lies in the pagan reliance on the eternal return of the natural cycle, forever opposed to the apocalyptic break with nature of the Judaeo-Christian imagination. As the history

of early Christianity wore on and the hopes for an imminent apocalypse
wore off, the Christians instituted a calendar of ritual observances to
pass, so to speak, the time. These ritual performances are undertaken
by individuals, but their effect is "religious" in the sense that it binds
people together in a communal, social body. This binding can be politically inflected in different ways, and Frye suggests a certain affinity
between the symbolism of Christianity and a "political ideal of democracy" (*GC,* 101).

In passing from "Typology I" to "Typology II" Frye shifts gears from
"The Order of Words" to "The Order of Types," and the itinerary from
language to myth to metaphor to typology now begins again in reverse.
In his introduction Frye terms this a "double mirror" structure, precisely the phrase he used to illustrate the organization of the Bible. He
speaks of his own text as falling into this form as if "by accident," but
in fact *The Great Code* is the most cogently structured of all Frye's
books. For all its fearful symmetry, the *Anatomy of Criticism* might have
been organized equally well in a variety of ways. *The Great Code* proceeds from great things to small, from a theory of language to the
organizing structures of myth, to the texture of metaphor and the distinctly biblical idea of typology. The first of the two chapters really
only addresses the "idea" of typology, leaving the more sinewy details
for the opening of part 2, "The Order of Types."

What interests Frye in his second analysis of typology, broadly
understood, is the sequence of its phases, of which he discerns seven:
creation, revolution or exodus, law, wisdom, prophecy, gospel, and
apocalypse. Especially for the Christian reader, this series might appear
as something of a progression. But Frye prefers to think of it in terms
of a "wider perspective" that distinguishes any of the later phases from
its preceding one. Unlike the sometimes Byzantine phases of generic
cycles in the *Anatomy,* these phases of the Bible do constitute a sequence. There may be no other book structured quite like the Bible,
but its movement has a powerful narrative logic. From the beginning,
that logic is one of the Logos, for in Genesis "the forms of life are *spoken*
into existence" (*GC,* 106). Yet the Bible does not proceed beyond its
opening chapters before becoming more historical than logical. Its creation story begins with a paternal sky-god forming the universe ex
nihilo and then inventing, as the crowning event in a series of fiats,
man. And out of man, almost as an afterthought, woman. One of the
nagging questions about the Genesis account asks why the deity to
whom we are supposed to be devoted is so "intolerably patriarchal"

(*GC*, 107). At one level, the answer is simple: "God is male because he rationalizes the ethos of a patriarchal male-dominated society" (*GC*, 107). But Frye's interest goes beyond this rather obvious conclusion— obvious, that is, to a Blakean who believes that all deities reside in the human breast—to speculate why the sky-god father makes symbolic sense in terms other than the rationalization of an ideology already in place. At this more abstract level, the answer returns to the importance for the Bible in distinguishing its mythos from the rhythms of nature, with its cycles of fate and inevitability, common to the religions of Israel's neighbors. God has to be a symbolic father because the mother is always already Mother Nature. The absolute beginning of creation has to be distinguished from the biological or natural beginning that we know as birth.

But Genesis clearly has to account in some fashion for the natural world, and it is barely a few chapters into the Bible that man "falls" from a mythical higher level into the state of nature. The Fall brings with it a certain knowledge of good and evil, the two not being entirely distinct. The fall into nature is equally a fall into society, for with the expulsion from the Garden of Eden arises the "legal metaphor . . . that persists all through the Bible, of human life as subject to a trial and a judgment, with prosecutors and defenders" (*GC*, 110). But even with regard to the period before man begins to form social units of his own, Frye posits a dark reading of the consequences of language itself, even divine language: "to speak is to enter the conventions of language, which are part of human death-consciousness; so if we push the image far enough, we come to the possibility that as soon as God speaks, and transforms himself into a Word of God, he has already condemned himself to death" (*GC*, 111).

With the second phase, which Frye terms "revolution," roughly the period of Moses and the Exodus, the Bible increasingly addresses the historical problems of Israel rather than the cosmic and existential ones of man in general. God enters history through his revelation to Moses and promises to take the side of the Hebrews in their opposition to the Egyptians. Thus "history" is the struggle against oppression, a history that is to culminate in a future moment of redemption, whose concrete form can assume various shapes. In a revolutionary context, the word of God takes on an increased importance, with a concomitant emphasis on the ear rather than the eye. Moses may have survived a vision of God, but no one else is afforded even a glance at God's "back parts." The spoken word then is primarily a call to action, and in this respect the revolutionary phase of Exodus anticipates the classical period of prophecy, even though we refer to the great figures of that age as the "writing prophets."

In the face of political oppression on the one hand and a struggle against fallen nature on the other, it is not long before the Hebrews have to lay down their laws. In response to a time of extreme crisis, the Hebrews find it necessary to consolidate their common practices and beliefs through an authoritative codification of them. But the law is by its very nature general, and so is succeeded in the Bible's sequence by what is called "wisdom" literature, of which the exemplars are the Book of Proverbs and Ecclesiastes. Wisdom is, in Frye's characterization, "the individualizing of law" (GC, 121), the particular and pragmatic moment when a general law has to be related to specific situations. Wisdom comes to be defined in terms of tradition, dominated as it is by what Frye terms "the anxiety of continuity." Wisdom draws on the past for its power, but it is nonetheless future-oriented in its aspect as prudence, a source of answers to the omnipresent question of "What is to be done?"

This same question is asked, with even greater urgency, in the fifth phase of the Bible's sequence, namely, prophecy. If "wisdom is the individualizing of the law," then "prophecy is the individualizing of the revolutionary impulse" (GC, 125). Though many of the figures called prophets are little more than functionaries of the state, the authors or redactors of the Bible chose to focus on a number of prophets who spoke out against royal policies and were persecuted for it. The prophet's force depends on speaking with an authority beyond himself, and it is no small matter to come up with criteria for distinguishing between true and false prophets. No wonder, then, that the prophet—whose role is by no means simply to predict the future—often comes into his own well after the fact of his prophesying. Prophecy presents a more "comprehensive view of the human situation" (GC, 128) by conceiving of history not in linear fashion but as a "U-shaped curve" in which the present is usually at the bottom. Thus the importance in the Hebrew prophets of the motif of the "saving remnant," a type of the Messiah to come.

The "Old" Testament closes with the books of the minor prophets and the New Testament begins with the Gospels, accounts of the life of Jesus that are so thoroughly steeped in a reading of the prophets that they constitute "a further intensifying of the prophetic vision" (GC, 129). The distinction between the Old and New Testaments is often considered under the rubric of *pleroma* or fulfillment, but Frye prefers to emphasize the concept of *metanoia* instead. *Metanoia* suggests "a change of outlook or spiritual metamorphosis, an enlarged vision of the dimensions of human life" (*GC*, 130). The Ten Commandments of the Mosaic dispensation are not so much negated as given their positive transformation in a document like the Sermon on the Mount. Christ continues the prophetic legacy of the Hebrew Scriptures by taking up the stance of a public menace, "the one figure in history whom no organized society could possibly put up with" (*GC*, 133). Paradoxically it is this one intolerable figure who himself figures the identity of all mankind, the one who makes it possible to be "one" with God. Through the appearance of Jesus Christ what was once "Israel" is transformed into a universal kingdom of God, thus expanding still further the parameters of the biblical vision.

In the seventh phase of the biblical sequence God can hardly be thought to have rested. With the coming of the apocalypse, the Bible reaches the absolute limit of theological time and space, to say nothing of history. Though we tend to speak rather loosely of prophecy as "vision," for Frye "the Book of Revelation is not a visualized book in the ordinary sense of the word" (*GC*, 135). The vision recounted in the Apocalypse of Saint John the Divine comes more from what he "saw in Ezekiel and Zecheriah" than from "whatever . . . he saw on Patmos" (*GC*, 135). Frye distinguishes two different apocalypses within the Bible's final book, a panoramic and a participating apocalypse. The first is the spectacle of sublime marvels to come in the future "at hand," as it says in Saint John's text, with its dialectical separation of sheep and goats and the destruction of the cosmos as we know it. What Frye calls the participating apocalypse "begins in the reader's mind as soon as he has finished reading" (*GC*, 137). There is of course much less textual evidence for this second apocalypse, which is eminently Blakean in character. Blake could speak of *a* Last Judgment rather than *the* Last Judgment because, understood allegorically, it is an infinitely repeatable event. It occurs, Blake says, every time an individual rejects error and embraces truth. Nowhere more than in Revelation is it clearer that "the Bible deliberately blocks off the sense of the referential from itself" (*GC*, 137). The referential, that is, understood in terms of history. The apocalypse does present something of a "vision," as Frye observes in revisionary, radical Protestant fashion: it is "the way the world looks after the ego has disappeared" (*GC*, 138).

In some respects Frye's rehearsal of the sequence of biblical modes offers an account that could have been predicted: much of what is said is not new. But the tendency in such surveys is to see the succession of phases simply as a historical one. What distinguishes Frye's account is his attention to the relation between the various phases, the way each succeeding phase enlarges upon the scope of the preceding one. Not only does this make greater sense of the material at hand, it also helps explain the power of the Bible as a literary text in matters beyond those of doctrine and belief.

Reversing the trajectory of the first half of *The Great Code,* Frye takes up his second discussion of metaphor of the Bible. The principles involved are precisely those outlined in the essay on symbols in the *Anatomy.* The four levels of the mythological universe can be deduced from the Bible, as the same patterns of dialectical and cyclical organization apply. No image, Frye argues again, is in itself good or bad. Indeed, the Bible displays an almost rigorous counterpoint in playing positive and negative aspects of the same image off against each other. Water, tree, fire, even the serpent can each appear in its ideal or its demonic form. Frye discerns five "bodies of imagery" in the Christian Bible: the paradisal, the pastoral, the agricultural, the urban, and "the imagery of human life itself" (*GC,* 144). The painstaking categorizing of imagery has one striking result that sets the Bible apart from literary texts, even as it illuminates the way the latter function. Frye succeeds in demonstrating how "the body of Christ is the metaphor holding together all categories in an identity" (*GC,* 166). A hallmark of the apocalyptic text is, as Frye has often noted, that anything is potentially identifiable with anything else. This is true in spectacular fashion of the Christian Bible, with the qualification that all the identifications are anchored in the person of Christ. The Book of Revelation is at once the epitome and the most extreme version of biblical imagery, recapitulating a whole range of motifs and metaphors from the Old Testament (it has, Frye notes, almost no verbal links to the New). The artful but opaque prophecies of Saint John the Divine would be all but indecipherable were they not all ultimately referring to the Logos as their organizing principle.

Frye's second run at the topic of myth addresses in detail what can be called typology proper: the narrative and figural system of types and antitypes that form the recurrent patterns of the Bible, Old Testament and New. The broadest schema of biblical narrative is also its most typical, so the speak, for the U-shaped story that marks the Bible as a divine comedy occurs again and again in the two testaments. The general pattern is that of a fall from prosperity or innocence to some kind of bondage or disaster, personal or (more often) political, followed by a deliverance that restores the person or group to something resembling their original state or better. Thus Adam and Eve's fall in Eden and expulsion into the wilderness parallels the exile from the promised land into Egypt. Frye distinguishes many instances of this pattern in the Old Testament—thus doing away with the suspicion that typology is a Christian "invention"—and argues that the principal result of these recurrences is the identification of the similar persons or group. Thus Israel faces a series of hostile kingdoms and empires: Egypt, Philistia, Babylon, Syria, and Rome, all of which become symbolically identical. If this is largely implicit in much of the Hebrew Scriptures, it is much more clearly spelled out in the New Testament. Indeed, Frye suggests that the New Testament authors take great care in orchestrating the movements of the Gospel narratives to harmonize with the patterns already established in the Scriptures. He writes, for example, that the "Gospels could hardly have been more careful than they are to synchronize the Crucifixion with the feast of the Passover, to make it utterly clear that the Passion, as they saw it, was the antitype of the Passover sacrifice" (*GC*, 173). Frye's phrasing suggests the primacy of symmetry over historical accuracy, which is not surprising given that the Bible, as constructed and reconstructed in Christianity, resembles nothing so much as a romance: "The Christian Bible, considered as a narrative, has for its hero the Messiah, who emerges, as frequently happens in romances, with his own name and identity only near the end" (*GC*, 174). In this regard, among others, the sacred parallels the secular.

The romance of the Logos, if we may call it that, is the most comprehensive of romances, for it encompasses the conceivable limits of time and space. Beginning in heaven even before the creation, the path of the son of God moves through the phases of creation, incarnation, and death until it reaches the nadir in a descent to hell. This last moment in the itinerary rests on "weak" evidence in the New Testament, but Frye notes "that what fills out a scheme and is not mentioned, or is only doubtfully referred to, in the Bible is very apt to be supplied by later legend" (*GC*, 175). This explains the popularity of the medieval iconography of Christ's "harrowing of hell," which makes symbolic sense even if it has no scriptural authority behind it. From the nadir in hell, the movement turns upward toward the resurrection and then to the ascension back into heaven where the story began.

Just as the Bible contains numerous parallels to romance, from the slaying of the dragon at creation to the miracles of Jesus, so does it correspond at many points to the popular folktale. The emphasis on

Jesus as the firstborn son, for example, is crucial for structural and doctrinal reasons. Though we have little sense of the brothers of Jesus, Matthew is quite explicit about their existence, whose main function seems to confirm Jesus' identity as the firstborn. The history of the firstborn male as established in the Hebrew Scriptures condemns Jesus in advance to being a sacrificial victim as well as to living in isolation and exile before any restoration can occur. In this regard Jesus follows Israel, whom God calls his "firstborn." "This structural theme," Frye notes,

> reminds us of folktales where a great quest is to be achieved and a number of older brothers fail to do so before a younger one succeeds. It reminds us chiefly by contrast, it is true, because here it is not any human hero who achieves a quest: the hero, Israel, is merely granted a promise. But the narrative parallel is still significant. In the folktales we know best it is usually the third son or hero who succeeds, as the rhythm of three seems to provide the most satisfying balance between tension and resolution in a story.
>
> (GC, 186–87)

However much the biblical narratives resemble romances or folktales, they retain a certain difference from their secular counterparts by virtue of their incorporation into encompassing typological structures. One of the chief insights that a literary reading of the Bible can provide is that there is no other text quite like it.

Myth considered as an "order of types" is crucial for the way biblical texts tend to repeat, summarize, or epitomize. The life of Jesus, for example, unites in a single person the figures of priest, prophet, and king, even though these three kinds of authorities were quite distinct within the Old Testament. And a narrative like the Book of Job, in a different manner, can be seen as an epitome of the Bible as a whole, tracing in its brief compass the movement of the Bible from a struggle against a monster in the beginning to a miraculous restoration at the end: "Job seems to have gone the entire circuit of the Bible's narrative, from creation and fall though the plagues of Egypt, the sayings of the fathers transmitting law and wisdom, the flash of prophetic insight that breaks the chain of wisdom, and on to the final vision of presence and the knowledge that in the midst of death we are in life" (GC, 197). Most sacred texts, of course, do not rely on narrative nearly to the degree that the Judaeo-Christian Scriptures do, much less on an almost obsessive repetition and recreation of what is, from a certain point of view, a single story.

Frye's itinerary within *The Great Code* comes full circle with the closing chapter, "Language," returning to its beginning. But there is a difference within the repetition: the second essay is subtitled "Rhetoric," as opposed, for example, to the emphasis on grammar in the opening chapter. Frye's point of departure is the Book of Revelation, a book that reflects on and makes a theme of its status as a text, as witnessed in its admonition to the reader not to remove or add anything from or to it.[18] The emphasis on the sacred text is pronounced from early on in biblical tradition, with the Hebrews showing a marked devotion to canonical writing. As Frye says: "In general it was the heathen kingdoms that produced the really impressive temples and palaces, while the Israelites produced a book" (*GC*, 200). The actual composition of the Bible was so complex and so long a process that it forever disturbs considerations of it in terms of "authorship," "originality," and "inspiration." Frye can state bluntly: "There is no way of distinguishing the voice of God from the voice of the Deuteronomic redactor" (*GC*, 203). The Bible as it now exists, in its Hebrew or Christian versions, is clearly not the record of the actual words of God, the *ipsissima verba*, even if the book is so often considered "the word of God." That is to say, the Bible is a translation from the very start, a state of affairs only exacerbated by the fate of its subsequent "translations," understood literally. In the transformation from one language to the next, the translation takes on a life of its own, a situation in which the status of "original" and "translation" seems reversed. "It is a sobering thought," Frye comments, "that it is sensitivity to one's own language, not scholarly knowledge of the original, that makes a translation permanent" (*GC*, 208).

The tangled web that makes up the biblical text perplexes hermeneutic approaches that prize originality and authorial intention, but the problematic status of the text should suggest another tack for interpretation, one that takes the canonical shape of the Bible as its starting point. Scholars are able, for example, to discern within the "Book of Isaiah" the work of at least three different hands. But rather than taking this as a sign of the text's spurious unity, Frye would seize the occasion to make sense of the pattern of descent, bondage, and return within the text of the Bible as we have it. The real unity of the book lies in the coherence of its pattern, not in the intentions of its multiple authors.

It is no wonder that this intensely polyphonic text would give rise to a voice of authority that is "impersonal." The very notion of prophecy or inspired speech requires a sacrifice of the individual voice, and much the same is true of proverbs and wisdom literature in general. The emphasis within the Bible is primarily on the "word of the Lord" as spoken and heard. Frye notes that "what is said to be written by God's own hand in Exodus 32:16 is destroyed by verse 19. Jesus says that his words will outlast heaven and earth (Mark 13:31), but there is only one possible instance of his actual writing: Jesus traces something in the sand and if he indeed wrote something, the words were soon erased (John 8:6). Many of the prophets wrote or had their oracles recorded in writing, but the archetypal prophet is Elijah, who, whatever else he may have been, was clearly not a wirter" (GC, 213–14). The language of the Bible is, not so paradoxically, a language that seeks to be beyond writing, a text that seeks to transcend its textuality.

The extraordinarily complex history of the Bible's composition makes for what is, from one perspective, an extremely disparate text. The Bible is a mosaic, to invoke one of Frye's recurring puns, "a pattern of commandments, aphorisms, epigrams, proverbs, parables, riddles, pericopes, parallel couplets, formulaic phrases, folktales, oracles, epiphanies, Gattungen, Logia, bits of occasional verse, marginal glosses, legends, snippets from historical documents, laws, letters, sermons, hymns, ecstatic visions, rituals, fables, genealogical lists, and so on almost indefinitely" (GC, 206). Not only does the Bible display an almost bewildering array of genres and subgenres, but its exemplary units are short and discontinuous, like the parallel verses that structure Hebrew poetry or the pericopes that riddle the Gospels.

Is it possible then to speak of the "unity" of the Bible, given its varied generic texture? Frye characterizes the unity of the Bible as "imaginative" (GC, 218), which is not say "imaginary," as if the coherence of the text were in the eye of the beholder. The imaginative unity of the Bible is based on the metaphorical and mythical structure of typology, which links images and events dispersed through the history of the Old Testament and the New. This unity is reinforced by the gradual creation (and recreation) of a single voice of authority that speaks through a whole range of willing and unwilling vehicles, of which the prophet is only the most extreme example. Rather as in literary tradition as outlined in the Anatomy, the voice of biblical authority is "impersonal" (GC, 212). The Bible, however, is "more" than work of literature: its rhetoric is more oratorical, more intent on persuasion, than is the disinterested use of words specific to literature. A literary reading of the Bible reaches its boundary where knowledge ends and faith may or may not begin. But there can be no circumventing questions of language: the leap of faith cannot leap over the words of the text. This, then, is the greatest contribution of *The Great Code:* to insist on the omnipresence of rhetorical questions, as it were, and to begin to answer so many of them. "Every text," Frye observes, "is the type of its own reading" (*GC*, 226), and Frye's reading of the Bible is in more than one sense "anti-typical." Frye's revisionary reading is powerful and persuasive enough, in its attention to detail and its grasp of architectonic structures, to suggest that *The Great Code* takes its place among the great decodings of the book that stands "in the middle of our cultural heritage" and at the end of Frye's itinerary.

Chapter Seven
Conclusion

Keats, in a famous letter, claimed that Shakespeare had led a life of allegory and much the same could be said of Frye. Keats meant that Shakespeare's works were "comments" on his life, whereas Frye's "life" has in a different way been devoted to allegory, its theory and practice. Frye learned from his work on Blake how to read the "minute particulars" of poems by situating them in a vast network of myths and images largely derived from the Bible. Frye's work had its precedents in the anthropological studies of Sir James Frazer and others, but with respect to literary studies *Fearful Symmetry* virtually invented a mode of criticism that would have literature's mythical and archetypal structures as its primary subject. Already in *Fearful Symmetry* Frye had hypothesized that a rigorous reading of Blake as an allegorist would be the beginning of a "revolution" in the reading of all poetry. The Blakean principle that poetry is best regarded as "allegory addressed to the intellectual powers" informed much of Frye's subsequent magnum opus, *Anatomy of Criticism,* which began as a project on Spenser's labyrinthine, allegorical epic, *The Faerie Queene.* What started out as a "local" difficulty in finding the appropriate critical language with which to address the interpretation of Spenser was soon transformed into an encyclopedic task of a theory of literature, complete with a grammar, logic, and rhetoric of criticism.

Anatomy of Criticism, the principal of Frye's many achievements, has been read as the credo of "archetypal" or "myth" criticism, but it is manifestly much more than that. Reading Frye against his critics—or simply reading him patiently in the first place—one discovers that Frye not only describes but also advocates a multifaceted approach to literature that cannot be contained under the rubrics of archetypal or myth criticism. It is true that Frye's most distinctive contributions to the theory and practice of criticism have been in the areas of myth and archetype, but that hardly warrants the translation from a relatively personal achievement to a theoretical program. The *Anatomy* must be read as a whole, if one is to assess both the scope and the radical nature of what Frye has to say. Perhaps now that a certain vogue of archetypal criticism has come and gone, a more sustained and systematic rereading of Frye can begin.

In the *Anatomy,* Frye set out to provide literary criticism with a conceptual framework of its own, a critical vocabulary informed by principles derived from an inductive reading of literature, but one that would retain a certain autonomy from literature itself. The language of literature and the language of criticism never quite coincide. Especially at its most concentrated, in the form of poetry, literature resists translation even as it seems to demand it: criticism is the performance of that necessary but impossible act of translation.

Frye's theory of criticism as proposed in the *Anatomy* has by no means been adopted by the discipline as a whole, as has sometimes been the case for theoreticians in the natural sciences. But Frye did manage to clarify the theoretical issues at stake in the practice of literary theory, and Anglo-American criticism, as well as criticism in the West generally, is massively indebted to Frye's programmatic work, even when it seeks to go "beyond" the *Anatomy.* In the body of this text and its notes I have tried to draw attention to the many ways in which Frye's work has anticipated some of the most promising criticism being undertaken today. That is to say, many contemporary critics are the "antitypes" of Frye, whether they acknowledge it or not.

A reading of Frye in the sometimes obscure light of his critics during the decades since the publication of the *Anatomy* shows a more complex author than the one so often represented. No small number of "myths" have circulated in the name of the premiere exponent of myth criticism. The charge, for example, that Frye's theory of literature is a thinly veiled displacement of a theological or religious program turns out to be spurious, especially given the sustained treatment of the Bible in *The Great Code.* If it was not already clear in the earlier works why the Bible was so central a focus of Frye's attention, then his reading of the "Bible *and* Literature" in that late work shows once and for all that Scripture is "anatomized" because of its structure and influence as a text, not valued as a respository of doctrine. Frye may well be sympathetic to a certain Protestant reading of the Bible, but in his persona as a literary critic issues of belief and dogma do not arise as such.

A rereading of Frye also shows that his work is both more historical and less "aestheticist" than has been supposed. The most striking feature of the *Anatomy* is its "systematic" character, its relentless schematization of literary forms and critical categories. But, even within the *Anatomy*, "system" is not simply opposed to "history": the central concept of "displacement," for example, elaborated in the first essay, is nothing if not an instrument for understanding the mechanisms of literary change throughout history. Moreover, when one moves beyond the *Anatomy* to texts such as *The Secular Scripture*, with its utopian visions inscribed in class struggle, or *The Bush Garden*, with its long meditations on colonialism and regional culture, one must acknowledge Frye's awareness of the rootedness of literary texts in a network of social, political, and economic forces. Similarly, the charges of Frye's aestheticism turn out, on inspection, to be without foundation. The scandalous doctrine of the *Anatomy* that poems come from other poems has been misread to mean that the literary work of art exists in some transcendental space purified of all contamination with the merely historical. I have attempted to show how this reductive, indeed erroneous, view goes against the Blakean in Frye, with its vision of art as a liberating force in society, as well as against the demonstration of the way literary forms are first and foremost conventional constructs. Such conventions, even when their content may suggest an "escape" from society and history, are social and historical through and through.

The function of literature within society is not merely a matter of "academic" or theoretical concern for Frye. Much of his energy has been devoted to the furthering of education in the broadest sense. He achieved a status as perhaps the foremost Canadian intellectual of his generation and the even rarer status of a literary critic who is read by a broad public. This can in part be ascribed to Frye's "democratizing" tendencies, his desire to be clear and accessible, especially in the considerable number of his books that grew out of public lectures or radio talks. Frye saw no reason to cloak what he had to say in the jargon of a specialized discipline, nor to bury it with a mass of scholarly footnotes.

In a late interview Frye claimed that he saw no reason why his productive life should come to an end. Time may prove him wrong on that count, but there is no reason why the productive reading of Frye should come to its end. More than perhaps any literary theorist of his time, Northrop Frye taught critics how to think about literature and how to conceptualize their own activities as critics. The theoretical and practical writings of Frye continue to pose a challenge for the future of criticism, a future in part made possible by Frye's work, though one which remains as unpredictable as the encounter between a text and a reader.

Notes and References

Chapter One

1. It is perhaps no coincidence that *Fearful Symmetry* is also divided into twelve chapters, corresponding to the traditional number of books in epic structure.

2. On the "heresy of paraphrase," see Cleanth Brooks, *The Well Wrought Urn* (Harcourt, Brace & World: New York, 1947), 192–214.

3. Paul de Man, preface to Carol Jacobs, *The Dissimulating Harmony* (Baltimore: Johns Hopkins University Press, 1978), ix.

4. Frye pauses now and then to indicate to the reader that he is not simply stating his own beliefs, with a phrase like "speaking as far as possible from [Blake's] point of view," but stylistic considerations alone would be enough to dissuade one from pointing out every instance of paraphrase. See *Fearful Symmetry* (Princeton, N.J.: Princeton University Press, 1947), 150; further references to *Fearful Symmetry* in the text will be abbreviated *FS*, followed by page number.

5. On the reception of Blake, see the informative study by Deborah Dorfman, *Blake in the Nineteenth Century: His Reputation as a Poet* (New Haven, Conn.: Yale University Press, 1969).

6. *The Complete Poetry and Prose of William Blake*, ed. David V. Erdman, rev. ed. (Berkeley: University of California Press, 1982), 641.

7. *Anatomy of Criticism* (Princeton, N.J.: Princeton University Press, 1957), 5; further references to *Anatomy of Criticism* in the text will be abbreviated *AC*, followed by page number.

8. *The Complete Poetry and Prose of William Blake*, 730.

9. On the relation of allegory to hyponoia, see Angus Fletcher, *Allegory: The Theory of a Symbolic Mode* (Ithaca, N.Y., and London: Cornell University Press, 1964), 2 n.1.

10. *Lay Sermons*, in *The Collected Works of Samuel Taylor Coleridge*, ed. R. J. White (Princeton, N.J., and London: Princeton University Press and Routledge & Kegan Paul, 1972), 6: 30.

11. For a fuller reading of the Coleridge passage, see Paul de Man, "The Rhetoric of Temporality," reprinted in *Blindness and Insight*, 2nd ed. (Minneapolis: University of Minnesota Press, 1983), 191–93.

12. *The Complete Poetry and Prose of William Blake*, 544.

13. Frye is noted in Paul de Man's "The Rhetoric of Temporality," cited above, as a key figure in the critical revival of allegory in the mid-twentieth century. De Man and Frye both agree on the importance of allegory and on some aspects of the interpretive problems it poses. But they part company in

several ways. De Man resists, for example, Frye's tendency to subsume allegory under anagogy, which, in Dante's words cited by Frye, signifies "some portion of the supernal things of eternal glory" (*FS*, 121).

14. *The Complete Poetry and Prose of William Blake*, 565. Blake is playing here with the Latin root of "real" (meaning "thing"), saying, in effect, that what most people think of as real things are neither things nor real. One should also note that for Blake not only are mental things alone real, only mental "particularities" are real in Blake's sense. He writes: "What is General Nature? is there such a thing? What is General Knowledge? is there such a thing? Strictly speaking All Knowledge is Particular" (648).

15. Ibid., 565–66.

16. The classic study by M. H. Abrams, *The Mirror and the Lamp* (London and New York: Oxford University Press, 1953), includes a very informative discussion of the topic. A more recent attempt to trace the history of thought about the imagination in the Enlightenment and romantic era, James Engell's *The Creative Imagination* (Cambridge, Mass.: Harvard University Press, 1981), is regrettably unreliable on many instances of doctrine and interpretation. For an insightful philosophical treatment focusing on Hume, Kant, Coleridge, and Wordsworth, see Mary Warnock, *Imagination* (Berkeley: University of California Press, 1976).

17. In *The Marriage of Heaven and Hell*. See *The Complete Poetry and Prose of William Blake*, 38.

18. *The Complete Poetry and Prose of William Blake*, 617.

19. This goes precisely against the grain of the dominant views of prophecy in Blake's time. Samuel Johnson's *Dictionary* (1755), for example, lists only two meanings for *prophet*, both of which are included in what Blake calls the "modern sense" of prophecy, that is, prediction.

20. For many Christian poets, classical mythology functions as a kind of counterpoint to the Bible, even if it occupies a clearly subordinate position.

21. Blake continued to do illustrations of poetic works, such as Dante's *Divine Comedy* and the Book of Job, but it is clear, as Frye observes, that the end of *Jerusalem* was the virtual end of his poetic production.

22. Frye often notes, following Hazlitt, that the arts are not "progressive" in the sense that they improve. He does observe, however, that literary traditions tend to become more explicit, which is certainly the case in a highly self-conscious work like Blake's *Milton*.

Chapter Two

1. Frye never returned to write a book-length study of Spenser; indeed, only one essay is devoted to *The Faerie Queene*. One could say, rather reductively, that "Frye's book on Spenser" was written by many of his students, among them James Nohrenberg, *The Analogy of "The Faerie Queene"* (Princeton,

N.J.: Princeton University Press, 1976), and Patricia Parker, *Inescapable Romance* (Princeton, N.J.: Princeton University Press, 1979), one section of which is devoted to Spenser. Though Angus Fletcher was never Frye's student, his *The Prophetic Moment: An Essay on Spenser* (Chicago and London: University of Chicago Press, 1971) is also deeply indebted to Frye's work.

2. It is common among Marxist critics to seize upon this notion as idealist and aestheticist, much as they take Kant to task for the supposedly apolitical concept of the disinterested in his *Critique of Judgement*. But it will be abundantly clear that Frye's "formalism" is not a denial of historical forces at work in the production of poetry. An earlier example of a concept of "disinterestedness" enlisted in a politically progressive program is found in the work of Hazlitt. For a forceful reading of this aspect of Hazlitt's thought, see David Bromwich, *Hazlitt: The Mind of a Critic* (New York and Oxford: Oxford University Press, 1983), especially 46f.

3. In the "Polemical Introduction" and elsewhere, Frye is keenly aware of the fragility of rhetorical paradigms in the history of science. That is, even though literary criticism can be scientific, science is itself always rhetorical or literary in one of its aspects. The topic of the rhetoric of nonliterary prose will be taken up again toward the end of this chapter.

4. This aspect of Frye's work is noted in Geoffrey Hartman's "Ghostlier Demarcations" in *Northrop Frye in Modern Criticism,* ed. Murray Krieger (New York and London: Columbia University Press, 1966), 109–31. The essay is reprinted in Geoffrey Hartman, *Beyond Formalism* (New Haven, Conn., and London: Yale University Press, 1970), 24–41. The volume edited by Krieger is a superb collection, including as well essays by William K. Wimsatt, Angus Fletcher, and responses by Frye.

5. Elsewhere I have outlined this aspect of Frye's work in relation to contemporary structuralist and poststructuralist thought, in "Can the Centre Hold?: Northrop Frye and the Spirit of the World," *Essays on Canadian Writing,* no. #7/8 (Fall 1977): 214–21. Frank Lentricchia also juxtaposes and opposes Frye and Derrida on the rhetoric of centrality in *After the New Criticism* (Chicago: University of Chicago Press, 1980), 14. It may also be noted that, in Derrida's view, even the notion of difference in Saussure does not preclude a certain reliance on the "center" as an organizing principle.

6. René Wellek, "Destroying Literary Studies," in *New Criterion* (December 1983): 6. William Wimsatt makes a similar error in objecting to Frye's claim that his distinction between "high mimetic" and "low mimetic" is merely "diagrammatic," claiming that "evaluations, and diagrammatic evaluations, do obtrude all through these essays." See his essay "Criticism as Myth" in *Northrop Frye in Modern Criticism,* 101. But Wimsatt certainly misses his target in the case of "high" and "low" mimetic, which refer primarily to the sphere of activity of the characters and by no means imply that Frye prefers the high to the low or vice versa.

7. This is not to say that literature is produced in a classless society. Indeed, a principle of class division is built into Frye's modal categories, such as high and low mimetic.

8. The most common charge leveled against Frye, especially from critics of the left, is that of "ahistoricism." But the literal primacy of "history" in the *Anatomy,* as well as many remarks concerning class, technical innovation, and so on, complicate any simple charge of ahistoricism.

9. For a critique of Frye along these lines, see Tzvetan Todorov, *Introduction a la litterature fantastique* (Paris: Seuil, 1970), 13f. See also Christine Brooke-Rose, *A Rhetoric of the Unreal: Studies in Narrative and Structure, Especially of the Fantastic* (Cambridge: Cambridge University Press, 1981), 55. Brooke-Rose adduces some interesting examples from fantasy and science fiction that cannot quite be accounted for in Frye's scheme, but these hardly detract from the viability of it in general.

10. See the helpful chart prepared in Robert D. Denham, *Northrop Frye and Critical Method* (University Park and London: Pennsylvania State University Press, 1978), 4. This is one of Denham's many "visual aids" that help summarize the more schematic aspects of the *Anatomy.*

11. It should be noted here that one of Frye's contributions as a practical critic is to illuminate a given work by showing how it is a displaced version of an earlier one. Thus one aspect of Lord Jim is suddenly clarified by observing his descent from the miles gloriosus, the braggart soldier. But see Wimsatt's objection to the infelicity of observations along these lines in *Northrop Frye in Modern Criticism,* 95–96. Frye's literary-historical genealogies and analogies tend to be more problematic in his analyses of societal issues. I will return to this point in chapter 4.

12. In this respect, Frye follows the example of Hegelian aesthetics, where several of the categories function both historically and "systematically," that is, purely by its difference from other categories in the system, irrespective of chronology.

13. Frye notes this cyclical movement apropos of numerous twentieth-century writers, but this does not mean, as some have suggested, that his vision of history is cyclical in the sense of a Nietzschean "eternal return of the same." Indeed, it is this aspect of Nietzsche's thought that Frye finds least profound.

14. This question will be taken up in more detail in chapter 3.

15. The phrase is a partial tautology, since the word "polysemous" is Greek for "many meanings." A principal source for the theory of fourfold meaning is Dante's "Letter to Can Grande." The standard study on the general topic in medieval thought is by Henri de Lubac, *Exegese medievale: les quatre sens de l'ecriture,* 4 vols. (Paris: Aubier, 1959–64). See also Erich Auerbach, "Figura," in *Scenes from the Drama of European Literature,* rpt. (Gloucester, Mass: Peter Smith, 1973), 11–76.

16. It is the insight of Locke, in his *Essay upon Human Understanding*, that words do not directly represent things but stand for the ideas of things within the mind. Somewhat along the same lines, the linguist Ferdinard de Saussure in his *General Course in Linguistics* divides the sign into signifier and signified, the latter being not a thing but a concept.

17. For a complementary view of the "mathematical" form of the aesthetic, see Paul de Man, "Aesthetic Formalization in Kleist," in *The Rhetoric of Romanticism* (New York: Columbia University Press, 1984), 263–90.

18. John Fekete reads ominous political overtones into words like "surrender" here to argue that Frye's is a discourse of capitulation. But the surrender Frye refers to here is a temporary one, moreover, one which has nothing to do with the quite different exigencies of practical politics. See John Fekete, *The Critical Twilight: Explorations in the Ideology of Anglo-American Literary Theory from Eliot to McLuhan* (London, Henley, and Boston: Rouledge & Kegan Paul, 1977), especially the chapter on Frye.

19. Thus, depending on where one looks in Frye, one can find that literature in general is characterized as allegorical or ironic. At one level of abstraction, allegory and irony are virtually indistinguishable. For a superb essay on the identity and difference of allegory and irony, see Paul de Man, "The Rhetoric of Temporality," 187–228.

20. The relations between literature, education, and society will be addressed in greater detail in chapter 4.

21. It is partly because of the archetypal character that a work can achieve "greatness" but the process works both ways. A "great" work tends to become archetypal, at least in retrospect, because it will engender other works in imitation of it.

22. For a brief, programmatic argument against the organizing concept of a center for language, see Jacques Derrida, "Structure, Sign, and Play in the Discourse of the Human Sciences" in *Writing and Difference* (Chicago: University of Chicago Press, 1978), 278–93.

23. For an example of a reductive version of this aspect of Frye's program, see Terry Eagleton, *Literary Theory: An Introduction* (Minneapolis: University of Minnesota Press, 1983), 93f.

24. For Frye's reading of *A Vision*, see "The Rising of the Moon," in *Spiritus Mundi: Essays on Myth, Literature and Society* (Bloomington and London: Indiana University Press, 1976), 245–74.

25. Wimsatt, "Northrop Frye: Criticism as Myth," in *Northrop Frye in Modern Criticism*, ed. Murray Krieger, 91.

26. Frye's insight here and in the fourth essay on genre anticipates much recent work, especially in structuralism and poststructuralism, on the rhetorical texture of nonliterary discourses such as philosophy and history. Hayden White's *Metahistory: The Historical Imagination in Nineteenth-Century Europe* (Baltimore and London: Johns Hopkins University Press, 1973), for example,

is deeply and explicitly indebted to Frye. I shall return to this topic in Frye, and its misunderstanding by certain critics, when discussing the fourth essay of the *Anatomy*.

27. See once more Wimsatt's essay "Criticism as Myth," in *Northrop Frye in Modern Criticism*, 102f.

28. This aspect of Shakespearean comedy is treated at greater length in *A Natural Perspective and The Myth of Deliverance*.

29. The topic of romance in Frye's work is taken up in greater detail in the next chapter but the structure of the *Anatomy* necessitates a brief consideration here.

30. On the reduction of rhetoric to the study of tropes, see Gerard Genette, "Rhetoric Restrained," in *Figures of Literary Discourse*, trans. Alan Sheridan (New York: Columbia University Press, 1982), 103–26. The relation between rhetoric and persuasion is a major preoccupation of the later work of Paul de Man. On the insufficiency of tropes and figures as the paradigm for literary language, see, for example, "Shelley Disfigured," in *Deconstruction and Criticism* (New York: Seabury, 1979), 39–73. The essay also appears in *The Rhetoric of Romanticism*, 93–123.

31. For a similar critique of uncritical notions of musicality with regard to prose, see the introduction to William K. Wimsatt, Jr., *The Prose Style of Samuel Johnson* (New Haven, Conn.: Yale University Press, 1941).

32. Frye later wrote a superb article extending the material from these pages of the *Anatomy*. See his "Charms and Riddles" in *Spiritus Mundi* (Bloomington and London: Indiana University Press, 1976), 123–47.

33. The notion of a dichotomy of abstract and concrete being resolved in the aesthetic is a position indebted to German idealist aesthetics, especially in Schelling's *System des transzendentalen Idealismus (System of Transcedental Idealism)*. Schelling's work became known in the English-speaking tradition largely through the writing (and plagiarism) of Coleridge. For a more contemporary view of the concrete universal that is compatible with Frye's, see William K. Wimsatt, Jr., "The Concrete Universal," in *The Verbal Icon: Studies in the Meaning of Poetry* (Lexington: The University Press of Kentucky, 1954), 69–83.

34. For a more extensive essay on the function of the anatomy with the *Anatomy*, see Louis Mackey, "Anatomical Curiosities: Northrop Frye's Theory of Criticism" in *Texas Studies in Language and Literature* 23, no. 3 (Fall 1981): 449–81.

35. Frye's work in this regard anticipates much of structuralist and poststructuralist thought on the rhetoric of philosophy. For one example, see the magisterial essay by Jacques Derrida, "White Mythology," in *Margins of Philosophy*, trans. Alan Bass (Chicago: University of Chicago Press, 1982), 207–71.

36. Frank Lentricchia, *After the New Criticism* (Chicago: University of

Chicago Press, 1980), 25. To make matters worse, this passage is cited in John Richetti (in an otherwise valuable book) as a "keenly skeptical rendering" of Frye's position. See his *Philosophical Writing: Locke, Berkeley, Hume* (Cambridge, Mass., and London: Harvard University Press, 1983), 1.

37. Among numerous objections to this statement of Frye's, see, for example, John Fekete, *The Critical Twilight,* 110.

38. Marcuse's position on the emancipatory role of art is elaborated in *The Aesthetic Dimension: Towards a Critique of Marxist Aesthetics* (Boston: Beacon Press, 1978).

Chapter Three

1. *The Secular Scripture* (Cambridge, Mass., and London: Harvard University Press, 1976), 23; further references to *The Secular Scripture* in the text will be abbreviated *SS,* followed by page number.

2. This is in fact the project of Fredric Jameson, who acknowledges his debt to Frye's studies of romance in "Magic Narratives: On the Dialectical Use of Genre Criticism," in *The Political Unconscious: Narrative as a Socially Symbolic Act* (Ithaca, N.Y., and London: Cornell University Press, 1981), 103–50. For a reading of romance that mediates between Frye's and Jameson's, see Patricia Parker, *Inescapable Romance* (Princeton, N.J.: Princeton University Press, 1979).

3. Compare the extravagant claim by Frye that "It is part of the critic's business to show how all literary genres are derived from the quest myth. . . ." See "The Archetypes of Literature," in *Fables of Identity* (New York: Harcourt, Brace & World, 1963), 17.

4. In the history of biblical criticism, it is precisely at the moment when faith in literal-historical interpretation of Scripture is shaken that the study of the Bible as a literary text begins. This shift in intellectual history is well charted in Hans Frei, *The Eclipse of Biblical Narrative* (New Haven, Conn., and London: Yale University Press, 1974). The consequences for literature of the late eighteenth and nineteenth centuries are taken up in E. S. Shaffer's suggestive study *"Kubla Khan" and "The Fall of Jerusalem": The Mythological School in Biblical Criticism and Literature, 1770–1880* (Cambridge: Cambridge University Press, 1975). Frye's reading of the Bible is indebted, though not always directly, to this tradition of "myth criticism," which begins in the middle to late eighteenth century with Lowth, Eichhorn, Herder, and others.

5. Frye's interpretation of Aristotle is still not a dominant one, though much of contemporary criticism has caught up with Frye's insight. At the time of the writing of the *Anatomy,* the dominant oppositional view was expressed in a work like Erich Auerbach's *Mimesis,* trans. Willard R. Trask (Princeton, N.J.: Princeton University Press, 1953).

6. Numerous Marxist critics of Frye, such as Terry Eagleton and John Fekete, have objected to what they call his "closed poetic universe." But the constraints of having to write within the conventions of a certain genre (to say nothing of conventions of grammar, diction, and so forth) do not imply the politically conservative stance that is often falsely ascribed to Frye through a mistranslation from literary to political categories.

7. The concept of "literariness"—whatever it is that makes literature literature—has been the object of much study and contention from the Russian and Prague formalists (Shklovsky, Eichenbaum, Jakobson) of the early twentieth century to the semioticians (Barthes, Riffaterre) of today. On this topic in Russian formalism, see the study by Victor Ehrlich, *Russian Formalism: History-Doctrine*, 3d. ed. (New Haven, Conn., and London: Yale University Press, 1981).

8. Frye had originally proposed *The Bottomless Dream* as the title for his study of Shakespearean romance and comedy, the book that was published as *A Natural Perspective*. The references in the title are more to Bottom the character from *A Midsummer Night's Dream* and to the sense of the "unending" movement of romance than to its "anatomical" sense, which is clearly what Frye's publisher had feared.

9. The word "riddle" is linked etymologically with the word "read." We will return to the problem of reading in romance shortly. For a fuller study of the riddle as genre and motif, see again Frye's excellent essay "Charms and Riddles," in *Spiritus Mundi: Essays on Literature, Myth, and Society* (Bloomington and London: Indiana University Press, 1976), 123–47.

10. For a provocative reading of the "critical romance" ranging throughout Frye's work, see Daniel T. O'Hara, *The Romance of Interpretation: Visionary Criticism from Pater to De Man* (New York: Columbia University Press, 1985), especially chapter 5.

11. For a fuller reading that addresses the relations between literary and political aspects of Morris's work, see Frye's important essay "The Meeting of Past and Future in William Morris," in *Studies in Romanticism* 21 (Fall 1985): 303–18.

12. Henry James, *Hawthorne,* ed. Tony Tanner (London and Toronto: Macmillan, 1967), 73.

13. For a fuller treatment of the poetic quest in romanticism, see Harold Bloom, "The Internalization of Quest Romance," in *The Ringers in the Tower* (Chicago: University of Chicago Press, 1971), 13–35. Bloom's early work is much indebted to Frye, as is most explicit in his study *Shelley's Mythmaking* (New Haven, Conn.: Yale University Press, 1959).

14. The romances, it should be pointed out, were "popular" in the sense that the roots of their stories are in folktale, rather than myth proper or in history.

15. Frye's position on the biographical criticism of the Shakespeare in-

dustry is clearest in his study of the Shakespearean sonnets, "How True a Twain," in *Fables of Identity* (New York: Harcourt Brace & World, 1963), 88–106.

16. Northrop Frye, *A Natural Perspective: The Development of Shakespearean Comedy and Romance* (New York: Columbia University Press, 1965), 7.

17. Frye observes that Shakespeare's "chief motive in writing, apparently, was to make money, which is the best motive for writing yet discovered, as it creates exactly the right blend of detachment and concern." See *A Natural Perspective*, 38.

18. Ibid., 30.

Chapter Four

1. Thus literature is for Frye, as it is for Adorno, autonomous to a considerable degree, at the same time that it is always a social fact (*fait social*). For Adorno's fullest exposition of this dual character of art, see his *Aesthetic Theory*, trans. C. Lenhardt (London: Routledge & Kegan Paul, 1984).

2. "The Responsibilities of the Critic" in *Modern Language Notes* 91 (1976); 808.

3. The CCF is the forerunner of the New Democratic Party, which remains democratic-socialist in character. Founded in the early years of the depression, the party in its Regina Manifesto called for nothing less than the eradication of capitalism. On this and other matters of Canadian history, readers, especially those unfamiliar with Canadian culture, may refer to Kenneth McNaught, *The Pelican History of Canada* (Harmondsworth: Penguin, 1976). For a more social than political introduction to Canadian history and culture, see George Woodcock, *Canada and the Canadians* (Toronto: Oxford University Press, 1970). For an excellent short view of the history of the church in Canada, see Harold Innis, "The Church in Canada," in *Essays in Economic History* (Toronto: University of Toronto Press, 1956), 383–93. On the tradition of Protestant dissent and the rise of Methodism in England, see the classic study by E. P. Thompson, *The Making of the English Working Class* (Harmondsworth: Penguin, 1968).

4. For Frye's retrospective account of his years as a writer and editor for the *Canadian Forum*, see "Rear View Crystal Ball," *Canadian Forum* 50 (1970): 54–55. This issue contains a number of illuminating accounts of moments in the history of the *Forum* by Ramsay Cook, Milton Wilson, and others. Cook speaks of the *Forum* losing its bearings in the fifties, presumably in the wake of Frye's term as editor after 1952. He notes, however, that the periodical was "still in the CCF camp."

5. One has to include "the arts" here because many of Frye's early reviews were devoted to music, painting, ballet, and film as well as to literature and criticism. For a complete listing of Frye's writings of the period, includ-

ing unsigned editorials in the *Canadian Forum,* see the very helpful bibliography by Robert Denham, *Northrop Frye* (Metuchen, N.J.: Scarecrow Press, 1974).

6. It should be noted that hardly any of Frye's writing is of a specialized, scholarly mold. Indeed he boasts that he is the sort of "scholar" who could not even find the Public Records Office. I shall return in the following chapter to the importance of the review as one mode of Frye's criticism.

7. The classic statement on how there can be no society without language and no language without society is found in Rousseau's *Second Discourse.*

8. For an exemplary reading of this problematic in the work of Descartes, see Jacques Derrida, "Languages and Institutions of Philosophy," in *Recherches Semiotiques/Semiotic Inquiry,* vol. 4, no. 2 (June 1984):92f., especially the first two sections. It should be pointed out that Derrida makes clear in the elaboration of his reading that the "way" is not simply a "metaphor."

9. Northrop Frye, *The Critical Path: An Essay on the Social Context of Literary Criticism* (Bloomington: Indiana University Press, 1971), 13. All further references to *The Critical Path* in this chapter will be given parenthetically in the body of the text. The phrases "middle life" and "dark wood" both allude to the opening lines of Dante's *Divine Comedy.* As is customary with such comparisons in Frye, the parallel between Frye the author and Dante the pilgrim is more ironic than self-glorifying.

10. See Geoffrey Hartman, "Ghostlier Demarcations: The Sweet Science of Northrop Frye," in *Beyond Formalism* (New Haven, Conn., and London: Yale University Press, 1971), 24–41. The phrase "the sweet science" comes from the final line of Blake's *Vala.*

11. Frye is sparing in his references to specific Marxist critics, though his generalization certainly holds for much of doctrinaire Marxist criticism. But there are important exceptions to the rule, such as Georg Lukács's *The Historical Novel* (Harmondsworth: Penguin, 1962), Fredric Jameson's *Marxism and Form* (Princeton, N.J.: Princeton University Press, 1971), the same author's *The Political Unconscious* (Ithaca, N.Y.: Cornell University Press, 1981), and Pierre Macherey's *A Theory of Literary Production,* trans. Geoffrey Wall (London: Routledge & Kegan Paul, 1978). Each of these works is well aware of the generic mediations of content.

12. For a classic statement on the possibilities and problems involved in writing literary history, see René Wellek and Austin Warren, *Theory of Literature,* 3d. ed. (New York: Harcourt, Brace & World, 1970), especially chapter 19.

13. Vico has been an important presence for a number of contemporary critics as distinct as Northrop Frye, Edward Said, Harold Bloom, and Hayden White. An excellent translation of Vico's magnum opus, *The New Science,* is that by Thomas Goddard Bergin and Max Harold Fisch (Ithaca, N.Y., and London: Cornell University Press, 1968). Vico's influence leads in several di-

rections, including the itinerary of socialist historiography. It is no accident that Edmund Wilson in his account of this tradition, in *To the Finland Station* (New York: Doubleday and Anchor, 1940), begins with an account of Marx's reading of Vico. For another, related appeal to Vico in Frye's work, see his important essay "The Responsibilities of the Critic," *Modern Language Notes* 91 (1976): 787–813.

14. Vico writes: "There must in the nature of human institutions be a mental language common to all nations, which uniformly grasps the substance of things feasible in human social life and expresses it with as many diverse modifications as these same things may have diverse aspects" (*The New Science*, 67: paragraph 161).

15. I will return to the example of Frye's analysis of the events surrounding the People's Park affair in Berkeley as one instance of such mythologizing.

16. Frye does not often use the word "ideology," but he remarks later on in *The Critical Path*: "Many of my readers would call what I am calling a myth of concern an ideology, and though, as I have indicated, I have specific reasons for using the term myth, those who prefer ideology may substitute it in most contexts" (*CP*, 112).

17. Frye does not dwell on the generic aspects of the defense, but for a valuable treatment of the genre in the Renaissance, including a chapter on Sidney, see Margaret W. Ferguson, *Trials of Desire: Renaissance Defences of Poetry* (New Haven, Conn., and London: Yale University Press, 1983). See also the excellent section on the *Defence* entitled "Sidney's Feigned Apology," in Ronald Levao, *Renaissance Minds and Their Fictions* (Berkeley: University of California Press, 1984), 134–56.

18. To teach by fable is not necessarily opposed to the spirit of religion. Frye follows a long tradition of Christian hermeneutics, at least from Augustine onward, which finds merit in the difficulty of interpreting texts whose messages or morals are not immediately clear. Luther considered Aesop's *Fables* the most valuable book after the Bible. (In the passage just cited from Frye, fable is understood in the broad sense of fiction.)

19. For a detailed view of the Berkeley student protests in the context of the larger American movement, see the neglected study by the philosopher John Searle, *The Campus War: A Sympathetic Look at the University in Agony* (New York and Cleveland: World, 1971).

20. Frye is doing something more here than pointing out that Locke, Rousseau, and others wrote explicitly about education. His contention is that their political myths imply a theory of education, even when the topic is not expressly addressed.

21. The word *spiritual* here has religious connotations but it is by no means limited to that narrow sense. Frye's spirit is somewhat like Hegel's *"Geist,"* which means intellect as much as spirit in the restricted, religious sense.

22. William Hazlitt, "My First Acquaintance with Poets," in *Selected Writings*, ed. Ronald Blythe (Harmondsworth: Penguin, 1970), 52.

23. The manuscript of Frye's address on the occasion of an honorary degree being presented to Prime Minister Diefenbaker is found in file "D" of the manuscript collection at the E. J. Pratt Library of Victoria College.

24. Frye's address at Carleton University, 17 May 1957, was entitled "Culture and the National Will" and is also found in file "D" of the Pratt Library's manuscript collection.

25. *Fearful Symmetry*, 420.

26. "Criticism, Visible and Invisible," in *The Stubborn Structure* (Ithaca, N.Y.: Cornell University Press, 1970), 87.

27. See the opening essay of *The Stubborn Structure*, "The Instruments of Mental Production," 7.

28. Ibid., 21. This is a recurring theme in Frye's writings. For another example see "The Definition of a University," in *Divisions on a Ground: Essays on Canadian Culture*, ed. James Polk (Toronto: Anansi, 1982), 148. Here Frye says "what appears to be real society is not real society at all, but only the transient appearance of society. The permanent form of human society is the form which can only be studied in the arts and sciences."

29. *The Stubborn Structure*, 21.

Chapter Five

1. *The Bush Garden: Essays on the Canadian Imagination* (Toronto: Anansi, 1971), 122; further references to *The Bush Garden* in the text will be abbreviated *BG*, followed by page number(s).

2. Hartman's remark paraphrases S. H. Butcher's comment that Aristotle can be described as "a Greek summing up Greek experience." See Hartman's excellent essay "Ghostlier Demarcations," in *Northrop Frye in Modern Criticism*, 109.

3. *Divisions on a Ground: Essays on Canadian Culture*, 121.

4. In this regard, it is interesting to read the memoir/hommage by Margaret Atwood that acknowledges the power of Frye's teaching even as it rejects the notion of the Northrop Frye school of poetry. See her "Northrop Frye Observed," in *Second Words: Selected Critical Prose* (Toronto: Anansi, 1982), 398–406.

5. Eli Mandel can rightly claim that Frye's work "has been extraordinarily influential in both criticism and poetry." See his valuable essay "Northrop Frye and the Canadian Literary Tradition," in *Centre and Labyrinth: Essays in Honour of Northrop Frye*, ed. Elanor Cook, Chaviva Hosek, Jay Macpherson, Patricia Parker, and Julian Patrick (Toronto: University of Toronto Press, 1983), 284–97.

6. Ultimately one would want to complicate the simple dichotomy between form and content, but the distinctions are relatively clear at this stage

of criticism. For a superb meditation on the shifting identities of form and content, see Fredric Jameson, *Marxism and Form* (Princeton, N.J.: Princeton University Press, 1971).

7. For a compatible view of the prehistory of modern Canadian drama, see Brian Parker, "Is There a Canadian Drama?," in *The Canadian Imagination: Divisions of a Literary Culture,* ed. David Staines (Cambridge, Mass., and London: Harvard University Press, 1977), 152–87.

8. *Divisions on a Ground,* 23.

9. For critiques of the thematic bent of Frye's Canadian writings, see the valuable title essay in Frank Davey, *Surviving the Paraphrase* (Winnipeg: Turnstone, 1983), and Paul Steuwe, *Clearing the Ground: English-Canadian Literature After Survival* (Toronto: Proper Tales Press, 1984), especially part 1.

10. Frye makes the point that any literary study is necessarily a work of comparative literature in his essay "Literature As Context: Milton's *Lycidas,*" in *Fables of Identity,* 123.

11. See W. Jackson Bate, *The Burden of the Past and the English Poet* (London: Chatto & Windus, 1971), and, among Harold Bloom's many books on the subject, his *The Anxiety of Influence* (New York: Oxford University Press, 1973).

12. "Haunted by Lack of Ghosts," in *The Canadian Imagination: Dimensions of a Literary Culture,* ed. David Staines (Cambridge, Mass., and London: Harvard University Press, 1977), 29.

13. *Divisions on a Ground,* 15.

14. See *The Bush Garden,* 135.

15. *Divisions on a Ground,* 25.

16. *Divisions on a Ground,* 71. Frye refers to "the colossal verbal explosion that has taken place in Canada since 1960."

17. *Divisions on a Ground,* 25.

18. For a provocative, revisionary history of Canadian culture in terms of "difference" (with special attention to the problem of colonialism), see Anthony Wilden, *The Imaginary Canadian* (Vancouver: Pulp Press, 1980)

Chapter Six

1. *The Great Code: The Bible and literature* (New York and London: Harcourt Brace Jovanovich, 1982), xviii; further references to *The Great Code* in the text will be abbreviated *GC,* followed by page number.

2. In general readers have been disturbed by certain skeptical, almost cynical, pronouncements throughout *The Great Code.* Frank Kermode maintains that despite the skeptical character of the text, "the driving force of this book is more mystical than skeptical." See his review, "The Universe of Myth," in *New Republic* (9 June 1982): 32. Kermode calls *The Great Code* an "amazing book" and a "work of very great distinction."

3. For an excellent treatment of the problems relating to the canonical

shape of the Old Testament, see Brevard S. Childs, *Introduction to the Old Testament as Scripture* (Philadelphia: Fortress Press, 1979). The "higher criticism" of the Bible, which focused on its composition and redaction, is not simply "opposed" to literary concerns. On the relations between the higher critics and poets in the late eighteenth and nineteenth centuries, see the valuable study by Shaffer, *"Kubla Khan" and "The Fall of Jerusalem": The Mythological School in Biblical Criticism and Secular Literature, 1770–1880*.

4. Translation begins as a historical necessity for Christianity but eventually comes to be something of a theological principle, as, for example, in Hegel's philosophy of religion, where the notion of the necessity of "spiritual" interpretation is linked with translation on the one hand and with the Holy Spirit on the other.

5. Though Vico is among the first to propose this notion, it would become a commonplace in the considerable literature on the origins of language in eighteenth-century thought, as in Condillac, Rousseau, and Herder. Among the rich studies of this topic, see Hans Aarsleff, "The Tradition of Condillac: The Problem of the Origin of Language in the Eighteenth Century and the Debate in the Berlin Academy before Herder," in *From Locke to Saussure* (Minneapolis: University of Minnesota Press, 1982), 146–209; Paul de Man, "Metaphor," in *Allegories of Reading* (New Haven, Conn., and London: Yale University Press, 1979); Jacques Derrida, *Of Grammatology*, trans. Gayatri Spivak (Baltimore: Johns Hopkins University Press, 1976), especially 165f.

6. This has much to do with the passage from oral to written culture. In this connection Frye refers the reader to the important work of Eric A. Havelock, *A Preface to Plato* (Cambridge, Mass.: Harvard University Press, 1963). See also Havelock's important collection of essays, *The Literate Revolution in Greece and its Cultural Consequences* (Princeton, N.J.: Princeton University Press, 1982).

7. The Elohim of the Hebrew Scriptures are the most obvious indication of a polytheistic culture. For a provocative discussion of monotheism versus polytheism, see Freud's classic study, *Moses and Monotheism* (1939).

8. For a recent articulation of the rise of modern science and the theory and practice of language on which it was founded, see Timothy J. Reiss, *The Discourse of Modernism* (Ithaca, N.Y., and London: Cornell University Press, 1982).

9. The theory receives its fullest expression in J. L. Austin, *How to do Things with Words* (Cambridge, Mass.: Harvard University Press, 1962).

10. Frye's attitude toward the work of Sir James Frazer, author of the monumental study *The Golden Bough*, is double-sided. He is indebted to Frazer for his pioneering work in anthropology on the codification of myths, but he distances himself from many of Frazer's conclusions. For example, Frazer determined after finding evidence of stories in countless communities of a universal deluge that in every case there must have been a local flood, whereas

Frye would read the same data as evidence of a tendency to mythologize the past. For an extended discussion of Frazer, see Frye's "Symbolism of the Unconscious," in *Northrop Frye on Culture and Literature*, ed. Robert Denham (Chicago: University of Chicago Press, 1978), 84–94.

11. The same suspicion of symmetry is found in one of the earliest "myth" critics of the Bible, David Friedrich Strauss. His work was influential in English letters, largely on the strength on George Eliot's translation of his major work, *The Life of Jesus Critically Examined* (1835).

12. On the tangled fate of the literal and historical senses of Scripture in theology and biblical criticism, see the valuable study by Hans Frei, *The Eclipse of Biblical Narrative: A Study in Eighteenth and Nineteenth Century Hermeneutics* (New Haven, Conn., and London: Yale University Press, 1974).

13. This does not of course mean that Frye's work is somehow "free" of ideology: no discourse is. But to some degree ideology can be recognized empirically, especially at a certain historical distance. ·

14. The chapter "Metaphor I" gets short shrift here primarily because much of the exposition recalls arguments form the *Anatomy* on the centripetal and centrifugal movement of the reading process as well as on the cyclical and dialectical principles in the structure of imagery.

15. This is no doubt one of the most contentious points in Frye's challenge to orthodox Christian (Protestant or Catholic) understanding of the Bible. Pascal is only one example among many theologians who thought that the truth of the Gospels depended on the truth of the Hebrew prophecies.

16. Frye notes here as elsewhere the crucial difference between identifications *with* and identifications *as*. For a somewhat similar "typology" of metaphor, see William Empson, *The Structure of Complex Words* (Ann Arbor: University of Michigan Press, 1967), especially the essays "Metaphor" and "A is B."

17. On the complexities of the Book of Revelation in relation to the Old Testament, see the excellent study by Austin Farrer, *A Rebirth of Images: The Making of St. John's Apocalypse* (1949), rpt. (Albany: State University of New York Press, 1986). On the literary afterlife of Revelation, see Frank Kermode, *The Sense of an Ending* (New York: Oxford University Press, 1967).

18. One version of the Bible prepared by *Reader's Digest* omits this injunction, thus blotting its editors out of the book of life. (I am grateful to Cathy Caruth for drawing this fact to my attention.)

Selected Bibliography

PRIMARY SOURCES

1. Books of Criticism
Fearful Symmetry: A Study of William Blake. Princeton, N.J.: Princeton University Press, 1947.
Anatomy of Criticism: Four Essays. Princeton, N.J.: Princeton University Press, 1957.
The Well-Tempered Critic. Bloomington and London: Indiana University Press, 1963.
The Educated Imagination. Toronto: Canadian Broadcasting Corporation, 1963; Bloomington and London: Indiana University Press, 1964.
T. S. Eliot. Edinburgh: Oliver and Boyd, 1963; New York: Grove Press, 1963, Rev. eds., Edinburgh: Oliver and Boyd, 1968; Chicago: University of Chicago Press, 1980.
Fables of Identity: Studies in Poetic Mythology. New York: Harcourt, Brace and World, 1963. Includes "The Archetypes of Literature," "Myth, Fiction, and Displacement," "Nature and Homer," "New Directions from Old," "The Structure of Imagery in *The Faerie Queene*," "How True a Twain," "Recognition in *The Winter's Tale*," "Literature as Context: Milton's *Lycidas*," "Towards Defining an Age of Sensibility," "Blake after Two Centuries," "The Imaginative and the Imaginary," "Lord Byron," "Emily Dickinson," "Yeats and the Language of Symbolism," "The Realistic Oriole," "Quest and Cycle in *Finnegans Wake*."
A Natural Perspective: Essays on the Development of Shakespearean Comedy and Romance. New York: Columbia University Press, 1965.
The Return of Eden: Five Essays on Milton's Epics. Toronto: University of Toronto Press, 1965; London: Routledge & Kegan Paul, 1965.
Fools of Time: Studies in Shakespearean Tragedy. Toronto: University of Toronto Press, 1967; London: Oxford University Press, 1968
The Modern Century. Toronto: Oxford University Press, 1967.
A Study of English Romanticism. New York: Random House, 1968.
The Stubborn Structure: Essays on Criticism and Society. London: Methuen, 1970; Ithaca, N.Y.: Cornell University Press, 1970. Includes "The Instruments of Mental Production," "The Knowledge of Good and Evil," "Speculation and Concern," "Design as a Creative Principle in the Arts," "On Value-Judgements," "Criticism, Visible and Invisible," "Elementary Teaching

and Elementary Scholarship," "Varieties of Literary Utopias," "The Revelation to Eve," "The Road of Excess," "The Keys to the Gates," "The Drunken Boat: The Revolutionary Element in Romanticism," "Dickens and the Comedy of Humours," "The Problem of Spiritual Authority in the Nineteenth Century," "The Top of the Tower: A Study of the Imagery of Yeats," "Conclusion to *A Literary History of Canada*."

The Bush Garden: Essays on the Canadian Imagination. Toronto: Anansi, 1971. Includes selections from "Letters in Canada" from the *University of Toronto Quarterly*, 1950–59; "Canada and its Poetry"; "The Narrative Tradition in English-Canadian Poetry"; "Turning New Leaves"; "Preface to an Uncollected Anthology"; "Silence in the Sea"; "Canadian and Colonial Painting"; "David Milne: An Appreciation"; "Lawren Harris: An Introduction"; and "Conclusion to a *Literary History of Canada*."

The Critical Path: An Essay on the Social Context of Literary Criticism. Bloomington and London: Indiana University Press, 1971.

The Secular Scripture: A Study of the Structure of Romance. Cambridge, Mass., and London: Harvard University Press, 1976.

Spiritus Mundi: Essays on Literature, Myth, and Society. Bloomington and London: Indiana University Press, 1976. Includes "The Search for Acceptable Words," "The University and Personal Life," "The Renaissance of Books," "The Times of the Signs," "Expanding Eyes," "Charms and Riddles," "Romance as Masque," "Spengler Revisited," "Agon and Logos," "Blake's Reading of the Book of Job," "The Rising of the Moon," "Wallace Stevens and the Variation Form."

Northrop Frye on Culture and Literature: A Collection of Review Essays. Edited by Robert Denham. Chicago: University of Chicago Press, 1978.

Creation and Recreation. Toronto: University of Toronto Press, 1982.

The Great Code: The Bible and Literature. New York: Harcourt Brace Jovanovich, 1982; Toronto: Academic Press, 1982; London: Routledge & Kegan Paul, 1982.

Divisions on a Ground: Essays on Canadian Culture. Toronto: Anansi, 1982. Includes "Culture as Interpenetration," "Across the River and Out of the Trees," "National Consciousness in Canadian Culture," "Sharing the Continent," "Conclusion to *Literary History in Canada* (Second Edition)," "Teaching the Humanities Today," "Humanities in a New World," "The Writer and the University," "The Teacher's Source of Authority," "The Definition of a University," "The Ethics of Change," "Canada: New World without Revolution," "The Rear-View Mirror: Notes toward A Future."

The Myth of Deliverance: Reflections on Shakespeare's Problem Comedies. Toronto: University of Toronto Press, 1983.

Northrop Frye on Shakespeare. Toronto: Fitzhenry & Whiteside, 1986; New Haven, Conn., and London: Yale University Press, 1986.

2. Selected, Uncollected Essays
"History and Myth in the Bible." Pages 1–19 in *The Literature of Fact*, edited by Angus Fletcher. New York: Columbia University Press, 1976.
"Haunted by a Lack of Ghosts." Pages 22–45 in *The Canadian Imagination*, edited by David Staines. Cambridge, Mass.: Harvard University Press, 1977.
"The Meeting of Past and Future in William Morris." *Studies in Romanticism* 21, no. 3 (Fall 1982): 303–18.
"In the Earth, or in the Air?" (review of Paul de Man, *The Rhetoric of Romanticism*), *Times Literary Supplement*, 17 January 1986, 51–52.

SECONDARY SOURCES

Atwood, Margaret. "Northrop Frye Observed." *Second Words*. Toronto: Anansi, 1982, 398–406. Hommage/memoir of interest for its reflection on Frye as a teacher and an "influence."
Cook, Elanor; Hosek, Chaviva; Macpherson, Jay; Parker, Patricia; and Julian Patrick, editors. *Centre and Labyrinth: Essays in Honour of Northrop Frye*. Toronto: University of Toronto Press, 1983. Contains numerous first-rate essays, some explicitly about Frye.
Cook, David. *Northrop Frye: A Vision of the New World*. Montreal: New World Perspectives, 1985. An examination of Frye's "liberal" social vision, by a political scientist.
Davey, Frank. *Surviving the Paraphrase*. Winnipeg: Turnstone, 1983. The title essay in this collection offers a critique of the thematic orientation of Frye's Canadian criticism.
Denham, Robert D. *Northrop Frye and Critical Method*. University Park and London: Pennsylvania State University Press, 1978. The first full-length study of Frye's work to 1977. Especially useful for its charts and diagrams of material from the *Anatomy*.
Fekete, John. *The Critical Twilight: Explorations in the Ideology of Anglo-American Literary Theory from Eliot to McLuhan*. London: RKP, 1977. Includes an uneven materialist reading of Frye, especially the *Anatomy*.
Krieger, Murray, editor. *Northrop Frye in Modern Criticism*. New York and London: Columbia University Press, 1966. An excellent collection of essays by Fletcher, Wimsatt, Hartman, Krieger, and others, with a reply by Frye.
Lentricchia, Frank. *After the New Criticism*. Chicago: University of Chicago Press, 1980. Good on Frye's work in relation to New Criticism but unreliable on his ideological positions.
Mandel, Eli W. "Northrop Frye and the Canadian Literary Tradition." *Centre and Labyrinth: Essays in Honour of Northrop Frye*, edited by Elanor Cook et

al. Toronto: University of Toronto Press, 1983. Helpful consideration of Frye's place in Canadian letters (including fiction and poetry).

Steuwe, Paul. *Clearing the Ground: English-Canadian Literature after Survival*. Toronto: Proper Tales Press, 1984. Spirited, iconoclastic treatment of the Canadian critical scene.

Woodcock, George. *The Meeting of Time and Space: Regionalism in Canadian Literature*. Edmonton: NeWest Institute, 1981. Good essay on an important topic for Frye's Canadian criticism.

BIBLIOGRAPHY

Denham, Robert D. *Northrop Frye: An Annotated Bibliography of Primary and Secondary Sources (Toronto: University of Toronto Press, 1987)*.

Index